LEAH CHASE

LEAH CHASE
Listen, I Say Like This

By Carol Allen

PELICAN PUBLISHING COMPANY
Gretna 2002

*The word "Pelican" and the depiction of a pelican are trademarks
of Pelican Publishing Company, Inc., and are registered
in the U.S. Patent and Trademark Office.*

Library of Congress Cataloging-in-Publication Data

Allen, Carol, 1945-
  Leah Chase : listen, I say like this / by Carol Allen.
    p. cm.
Includes bibliographical references and index.
  ISBN 1-58980-048-6 (alk. paper)
  1. Chase, Leah. 2. African American women—Louisiana—New
Orleans—Biography. 3. African Americans—Louisiana—New
Orleans—Biography. 4. African American cooks—Louisiana—New
Orleans—Biography. 5. Dooky Chase (Restaurant) 6. Civic
leaders—Louisiana—New Orleans—Biography. 7. Art patrons—United
States—Biography. 8. New Orleans (La.)—Biography. 9. Madisonville
(La.)—Biography. I. Title.
  F379.N553 C43 2002
  976.3'35063'092—dc21
                                                        2002009935

Photos courtesy Leah Chase
Recipes from The Dooky Chase Cookbook,
  published by Pelican Publishing Company, Inc.

Printed in the United States of America

Published by Pelican Publishing Company, Inc.
1000 Burmaster Street, Gretna, Louisiana 70053

To our daughters,
Robin Lynn Jones
~
Stella Chase Reese
and Leah Chase Kamata

To my mother, Coy Hart Allen, another woman who changes lives
around her

And to the memory of Emily Chase Haydel

*Memory, in short, is engraved not merely by the
life we have led but . . . by the lives of others, which can cut
into ours every bit as sharply as our own experience.*

—Anthony Lane

Contents

Acknowledgments

When a writer writes her first book-length work, she's like a marathon runner. I think she is the only person who can cross the finish line, but a number of people have prepared her for the event and encouraged her along the course. I owe great thanks to many people.

My good friends and cheerleaders Debra Gawron, Sandi Getler, Anna Hayes, Susie Morgenstern, Kathryn Seris, and Drusilla Walsh spent time proofing drafts and giving me excellent input.

Several professionals were patient and steadfast in answering my many questions and assisting me in finding necessary documents and materials: John Bullard, Alice Yelen, and Bill Fagaley at the New Orleans Museum of Art; N. Burris, the *New Orleans Times-Picayune* librarian; the highly competent, friendly, and accommodating professional staffs at the main branch of the New Orleans Public Library, Louisiana Collection; Williams Research Center of the Historic New Orleans Collection; the University of New Orleans Library; the Amistad Center at Tulane University; the staff at John Folse Company; and the on-line research staff at the Smithsonian Institute.

Friends and acquaintances in the literary world gave counsel and listened: Odile Hellier, Tom Kennedy, Diane Johnson, Jake Lamar, Angela Miller, and Heather Jackson.

New Orleans friends opened doors and kept me abreast of what was happening in the city while I was far away: Laura Claverie, Lee Brasseau, Joe De Salvo, and Marda Kaiser Burton. George Dureau, longtime friend and artist, graciously allowed me to use the photo portrait he took of me for my book jacket.

Dee Moses, who few know to be an unrelenting proofreader, gave my manuscript a thorough going-over prior to my turning it in.

Many friends and acquaintances of Leah Chase gave generously of their time, allowing me to interview them.

The members of the Chase and Lange families were patient and enthusiastic in their responses to my many questions.

My two computer gurus, Jean Claude Mazuy in France and Westley Annis in New Orleans, were lifesavers when my technical inaptitude reared its ugly head.

The people at Pelican Publishing Company made the actual publication of the book a pleasure: Dr. Milburn Calhoun, owner/publisher, who took a personal interest in my book; Cynthia Williams, editor, whose editing was professional and precise, yet allowed the book to remain my book; Stephanie Williams, publicist, who worked untiringly to promote the book; and Kathleen Calhoun Nettleton, whose early interest in the book motivated and inspired me to work diligently toward the book's completion.

One dependable person who knew how to ferret out information and involved himself completely, literally becoming my eyes, ears, and feet in New Orleans, although he did not always agree with my interpretation of information, is a good friend and superb researcher, and deserves a special thank you. Thank you, Al Kennedy.

Naima Laaoeur is a wonderful woman and my good friend who took care of my household so I could work.

Finally, this project would have been a lot more difficult and a lot less fun without Fred the Great.

Introduction

When Carol Allen asked me who was writing my life story, I said, "Now, there would be a tale." When she asked me to consider letting her write it and we started our interviews, I laughingly told my friends she might get three pages on me. Now, she's actually written an entire book.

Carol and I have spent hours and hours and HOURS together. She has sat in my kitchen while I've worked, followed me around when I've been invited to do various things, met and talked with just about everybody in my family, traveled to Madisonville where I was born, and met my family who still lives there. She has talked to friends, reviewed old taped television shows, and even came to one of my family reunions. We've had a lot of fun working on this together.

As one is living one's life, one doesn't have time, really, to reflect on all that has passed. In reading the words Carol has written, I have been able to relive some of my experiences. Some have made me laugh; some have made me cry. Many have made me reminiscent of moments I had forgotten.

Carol asked me more than once, "Can I use that?" I told her, "Anything I tell you, you can use. I have nothing to hide from anybody." I believe my feelings, words, joys and sorrows, and hopes and disappointments have been captured in this book. I recognize myself and my life in these pages, and I am happy they reflect my love for my family, my love for the people who have helped and supported me, and my love for New Orleans.

My hope now is that someone will read this book and say, "Leah did it like this. I think I can do it better."

Leah Lange Chase

LEAH CHASE

Family home, Madisonville

CHAPTER ONE

Madisonville

When it's cold in Louisiana, folks say, the cold cuts to the bone. Humidity hangs wet over the state, making the cold seem colder, wetter, and worse than, say, in Montana. Wintertime in Madisonville, Louisiana, was bone cold. When the rain on the dirt yards around the houses would freeze over, the kids would skate across the ice, in their shoes. Cradled between the Tchefuncte River and Lake Pontchartrain, Madisonville caught the cold, wet air from every side.

The area around Madisonville was known for its fishing, the river deep and enhanced by the abundant oak and pine trees. The river had plenty of perch and bass, and the lake was a natural source of crabs, oysters, and shrimp. Numerous cypress, willow, and gum trees shaded the river's edge in summer, and the marsh grasses, water hyacinths, and lilies created soothing, colorful landscapes. But winters were hard.

In January 1923, Hortensia Lange was about to give birth to her second child. Her first child, Claudia, had died at eighteen months. A pot of scalded milk turned over on her and she didn't survive the ensuing complications. This second child would be the first of thirteen to come, but only eleven of Hortensia's children would survive. Hortensia was not about to give birth to her baby in Madisonville. She would travel across the lake to New Orleans, where her mother lived. Babies weren't born in hospitals in those days; they were born by midwives, and Hortensia's mother was a registered midwife.

With a bundle of baby clothes she had made herself, Hortensia boarded the *Steamer Madisonville.* Black people couldn't sit in the upstairs part of the boat, where there was a wood-burning stove and oil lamps; they rode below with the cargo and the vehicles. So Hortensia huddled into a seat, isolating herself from the cold lake air as best she could, wrapped herself in a blanket, and prepared for the three-hour journey across Lake Pontchartrain. It was bone cold.

Leah Lange was born on January 6. She shared a birth date with a woman who would later become one of her most admired people: Joan of Arc. This coincidence of birth dates could almost make one believe unequivocally in horoscopes. The characteristics of courage, leadership, standing up for one's beliefs, and deep Catholic faith are qualities both women share.

Not much was happening in Madisonville, Louisiana, or Madison, as the locals call it, in 1923. Madison was a country town, and people didn't lack for much in the country. They had big vegetable gardens so they had enough to eat. Most families had at least a couple of hogs, maybe a few chickens. And then there was the Tchefuncte River, where anyone with a line and bait, and a bit of patience, could catch a mess of fish.

Although whites and blacks lived side by side, their lives were segregated. The white Catholics attended St. Catherine's Church, named for the wife of a wealthy local merchant, and the black Catholics attended the older St. Francis Xavier, given to them upon the construction of St. Catherine's.[1] Protestants, regardless of color, were considered second class.

Everything in Madisonville revolved around the Tchefuncte River, which was deep enough to serve as an ideal place for the shipping industry. The men in town were shipbuilders, ship repairers, boat captains, boiler tenders. The *Steamer Madisonville* transported travelers from New Orleans' West End to Madisonville three times a week. Most of the town folk congregated on the banks when the steamer docked. It was always an exciting event, enhanced by an ever-present small orchestra accompanied by a man named Nelson Jean who belted out catchy music on his banjo. It could be said that the *Steamer Madisonville* went on to bigger and better things. According to the *St. Tammany Historical Society Gazette,* it was sold around 1930 and used as a sightseeing boat in New York City, carrying passengers to the Statue of Liberty.

Charles Robert Lange was a ship's caulker. At home, after a long day of working on wooden ships, he worked his huge garden. He would give the best of his vegetables to neighbors or the good sisters of the Holy Family at St. Francis Xavier Catholic School. The rest would be for the family. After a supper of biscuits and cured ham and greens, he would drill his children, all girls, on telling the time, using a clock with Roman numerals. He made them memorize the alphabet forward and backward. When the lights were out and the eerie shriek of screech owls filled the night, he admonished his children to shush and not be afraid. After all, it was nothing but a bird. He prepared his children for life. "Anything can happen," he told them, "and you can achieve anything if you just pray hard enough." And pray they did.

The family Hortensia and Charles Lange were building in the early '20s would eventually number eleven: nine girls and two boys—Cleo, Eleanor, Grace, Sylvia, Yvette, Adonicia, Eula, Charles, Janice, Hayes, and of course, Leah. They were church-going people and Catholic to the core, always giving and sharing with others. Hortensia Raymond Lange despised unkindness. She once became upset when an obese lady who attended St. Francis Xavier Catholic Church stopped going because of the giggling and tittering in the congregation upon her entrance into the sanctuary, and when old Mr. Gandy, hunchbacked and "coal" black, sat in the rectory in the back rather than be belittled in the sanctuary for his dark color and deformity. Hortensia spoke openly about these affronts at home in front of her children. She hated discrimination in a time when the word had not yet been coined. When people criticized others, she hammered into her children her belief there was something good in everybody; you just had to look for it.

None of this was lost on Leah Lange. The generosity of spirit, the detesting of discrimination, the discipline for learning, and the courage to not be afraid all became manifest in the future Leah Lange Chase. Today these qualities funnel through to her children, her grandchildren, and her great-grandchildren, continuing the legacy of her parents.

From her domain, the Dooky Chase Restaurant at 2301 Orleans Avenue in New Orleans, Louisiana, "Miss Chase," as people fondly call her, stretches her arms far and wide to others. It is only partly because of this quality that she is widely loved and respected. At

Leah's parents, Hortensia and Charles Lange

an award ceremony held in 2000, a man in the audience told Leah, "So many people love you. I wish half as many people loved me." Leah believes she must do something good for someone else every single day of her life. On May 18, 1998, when granting her the Loving Cup Award—the most prestigious citizen's award in New Orleans, given by the *New Orleans Times-Picayune* to honor someone who gives without expectation of reward—publisher Ashton Phelps said, "If Leah Chase were the average citizen, Louisiana would be a dream state."

Leah doesn't get back to Madisonville as often as she'd like. One of her sisters lives in the old homestead. Another lives in a home surrounded by towering pines, and her brothers, much younger, live nearby and spend their spare time hunting and fishing. When the family gets together, laughter prevails, stories are told, and tables groan under pots of steaming gumbo, chock-full of veal, shrimp, and *chaurice*.[2]

Tales about their parents are popular. Their father's corny fishing jokes are notorious: "They were biting so much today. Why, I had to go hide behind a tree to bait my hook! . . . Man said he caught a fish as big as a whale. A whale? I use a whale for bait. . . . How big was that fish? That fish was so big, when I pulled him out, the lake went down."

Not all memories are funny. Charles Lange was a disciplinarian and just the memory of his razor strap provokes raised eyebrows and sharp exhalations among the siblings. He never cursed or said ugly things, but when his daughters provoked him, he called them sobbing wenches. Hortensia, however, ruled the roost. Most often, it was disobedience to their mother that resulted in an encounter with their father's strap. And while Charles was easygoing and prone to ignore offensive comments from people, Hortensia was quick to put unkind people right in their place.

With her long straight hair and confident air, Hortensia strode barefoot about the packed dirt yard. She tended to her large family and to others in need. She sewed baseball uniforms for a whole team that had none, engaging her daughters to sew on the buttons and make the buttonholes. Her grandchildren don't remember her being especially grandmotherly. They recall her requiring them to be silent when they went fishing with her or be sent back to the house.

She was inventive, creative, and she loved nice things. When the children needed clothes, she took printed flour sacks and made dresses—beautiful dresses. She turned castoff wool coats wrong side out so that the good side was showing and made her children new coats. She was a genius with a needle and thread, but she hated to cook, except for baking bread. She loved to ply the dough, in and out, in and out, let it rise, then bake it in the wood-burning oven until it was toasty brown.

Every Sunday morning the Lange family dressed up and walked a half-mile to church. Hortensia was proud to see her children dressed nicely, and as poor as her family was, she worked hard to make them pretty clothes. Charles teased them, saying, "You worry too much about what you're putting on. If you had one suit, like I have, you wouldn't worry about what you put on. You'd just put on your one dress and go to church."

New dresses were an important part of every holiday. All Saints Day, although somber in its idea, was an exciting day for the family. Hortensia made the girls new dresses and the whole family spent the day at the cemetery, visiting the graves of the deceased and enjoying a picnic. Since the community was segregated, all the

Leah Chase and Ashton Phelps

Leah (middle row, second from left) *with her brothers and sisters*

black Catholics in town would descend upon the cemetery where their loved ones were buried. A lady who worked for the priest sold ice cream. Kids played; parents visited. The weather was still warm on November 1. It would be a lazy day, unlike the other days of hard work.

Thanksgiving Day was another jubilant holiday. There was food, food, and more food. At noon everyone would sit at the table and have a glass of strawberry wine and a bowl of gumbo. They would then leave the table and socialize, the women often chatting over hot, sudsy dishpans as they washed the dirty dishes and prepared for the next course. At two in the afternoon, everyone returned to the table and they stayed there until evening. A typical Thanksgiving dinner would include fresh pork roast, wild game that Charles had killed, oyster patties, oyster dressing, *petits pois* (garden peas), and cakes and pies. The canned petits pois would be the fanciest thing on the table. They weren't homegrown; they were expensive. Thanksgiving was a time for the family, hardworking and busy, to relax together, talk, laugh, and renew their contact with one another—and, of course, eat.

Christmas, on the other hand, was a full, busy week of festivities and required days of preparation. Families visited each other every day of the week between Christmas and New Year's Day, and food and drink were vital to the festive atmosphere. Cakes were prepared and stored, usually in the wire safe that hung on the porch outside the front room. Strawberry wine, a specialty of Charles Lange, was bottled from the thick crocks where it had fermented. Gas lamps lit the house. A gusty fire in a potbellied stove warmed the rooms.

BUTTER CAKE

1 lb. butter
1 lb. confectioners' sugar
6 eggs
2 ⅔ cups cake flour, sifted
2 tsp. vanilla

Preheat over at 350 degrees. Grease a cake pan.

With a mixer set on high speed, cream butter and sugar until light and fluffy. Add eggs one at a time, mixing well after each egg. Gradually add flour, mixing well and scraping down sides of mixing bowl. After all flour has been added, add vanilla and mix for 1 minute. Pour into greased cake pan and bake for 1 hour or until a toothpick inserted into cake comes out clean.

Church and the importance of prayer were drilled into the Lange children. "If you pray hard enough," Charles Lange taught his children, "you'll get what you need." Charles also believed in good works. He sent his daughters to iron for the nuns and to wash their dishes on Sundays after lunch. They had to polish the tall, heavy, brass candelabras in the church. Should friends or other family members become ill, Hortensia dropped everything to go help, and the girls maintained things at home. That's just the way it was. If Charles and Hortensia Lange knew of anyone who needed a helping hand, they mobilized their whole family. It was a way of life.

Charles' brothers kidded him about the pack of girls he'd produced. What good would they be? But nothing discouraged Charles about his daughters. Everyone, little or big, worked. They did their chores around the house, they did their homework, and naturally, they played.

The children loved to fly kites. Charles would cut thin strips of cypress and build the frames. The children mixed paste from flour and water and used it to stick paper to the light, wood frames. Then they tied razor blades to the tails of their kites. The objective was to move a kite close enough to the other children's kites to cut their strings, causing their kites to crash to the ground. Competition was keen.

Playing with dolls was another normal pastime. The dolls had porcelain heads, arms, and legs, and rag bodies stuffed with straw. What the Lange girls liked to do was clothe the dolls in the dresses they'd made themselves. They played tag, hopscotch, and a game called Pea-Put, which involved using a spinning top their father had made. The children drew a circle in the dirt and divided it in half. One half had a *P* written in it and the other had a *T*. Each child would then spin the top. If it landed on the *P*, the child had to put something into the circle. If it landed on the *T*, she took something out. The ante, so to speak, was usually candy.

When big jobs—such as making mattresses from the stringy Louisiana moss or killing a hog—came along, the girls' job was to baby-sit the younger kids. In strawberry season, getting in the fields and picking the berries at exactly the right time to insure a maximum crop was of prime importance, and the girls' help was needed. The prettiest berries were sold fresh and the others were used to make preserves and sweet strawberry wine. In fact, the children went to school only six months out of the year. The late spring months were for picking strawberries.

The road home from the strawberry fields ran beside a place called Palmetto Flat, a swampy area full of indigenous palmetto palms. It was a spooky area and the children scurried along quickly. The lingering rumor was that the Silk Lady would appear in the swamp. She was a ghost who first made herself known by the smell of watermelon; then the air would suddenly turn warm. Leah never saw the Silk Lady, but one of her sisters was sure that she did. One thing was certain: the girls would not go home and mention the

Silk Lady in front of their parents. Their father would have scoffed and their mother didn't want to hear any talk about ghosts.

When the Lange children weren't working at home, working for the sisters at the church, or picking strawberries, their activities revolved around the school. The nuns were always organizing something, and there was no question of not participating. Like so many families in those days, if the kids got into trouble at school, they got double trouble at home. When Sister Jules or Sister Josephine got upset with one of the Lange girls, she would walk the girl home, tell her parents, and wait until the child got a licking. The Lange girls learned to toe the line.

Leah quickly became a star. Smart for her age, she started school a year earlier than most. She always had the leading role in any school play. She knew the entire mass in Latin and, to this day, resents that she couldn't be an altar boy. Signs were already in the air that Leah Lange was going to be somebody to be reckoned with.

CHAPTER TWO

Moving On

There was no high school for black students in Madisonville. At the age of thirteen, Leah Lange did something that probably no other person of her race in Madisonville had ever done: she moved to New Orleans to live with an aunt and attend the all-girl Catholic school, St. Mary's Academy. Upon graduating at the age of sixteen, she returned home to get a job but quickly realized there were no jobs to be had except housework. The life Leah wanted to live was across the lake in New Orleans.

Leah's cousin, Mary, lived in New Orleans in the Seventh Ward and encouraged Leah to come live with her and her mother and work in New Orleans. Charles and Hortensia Lange were reticent about letting their daughter, who was only eighteen, take off on her own to the city. Charles, especially, worried about Leah's safety. As with most debates of this kind between parent and child, Leah won.

In New Orleans, she shunned the job well-brought-up Creole girls were expected to take, that of working in Haspel Brothers' sewing factory, and instead headed straight for the French Quarter. Nice girls didn't go to work in the Quarter, but Leah had a mind of her own and would follow her own instincts. A cousin helped her get a job at a laundry, where she lasted two days. She quit when she was reprimanded for working too quickly and efficiently. "There's plenty of time," her coworkers chided her. But Leah did not have plenty of time, nor did she have the disposition to waste the time she had.

Miss Bessie Sauveur hired her as a waitress at the Colonial

Leah graduating from St. Mary's Academy

Restaurant. Leah loved the work, loved watching what was going on in the kitchen, loved the clients, and soaked up as much knowledge about the restaurant business as she could, totally ignorant of the fact that she was getting on-the-job training for her life's work.

At the same time, Leah took other small jobs on the side, trying to get ahead faster. She was pretty, smart, witty, and had a nice figure. Naturally, she was popular, and she soon caught the eye of the talented and handsome Edgar "Dooky" Chase II. Five years younger than Leah and the leader of the Dooky Chase Orchestra, called the Pride of New Orleans in local papers, Dooky was a trumpet player and composer, and his orchestra played all over the Southeast.

It was only after Dooky and Leah married that Leah told her parents. She had covered most of her bases. Dooky was Catholic and Creole and they had married in the church, three important requirements for a girl like Leah. But he was a musician, a city boy, and younger than Leah and, had Leah's parents known about the wedding in advance, they wouldn't have approved. They would have worried that he wouldn't be able to make enough money to provide for their daughter. Among some in Leah's family, musicians were considered lazy people who lived only to play music and weren't considered stable people with steady jobs.

The Korean War virtually broke up the orchestra, and Leah and Dooky started their family. Dooky gave up his trumpet to help in the family business, a small sandwich shop, home of the famous New Orleans po' boy, where his father also sold lottery tickets.[1] As the children became school aged, Leah began helping in what was by then a popular, if small, family restaurant: the Dooky Chase Restaurant.

Miss Emily, Leah's mother-in-law, coiffed, bejeweled, and manicured, was always out in front with the customers. Plus, she controlled the money. The two Dookys, father and son, managed the bar. Leah quickly found her niche in the kitchen. Her French Quarter experiences, natural talents as a chef, ambition, hard work, and love of nice things were about to transform this small family restaurant into one of the most popular Creole restaurants in America.

Edgar Chase II and Leah Chase at the Viking Ball

CHAPTER THREE

Love and Sacrifice

What happens in a human being's life is largely a question of time and place. Had a president dallied with a twenty-five-year-old in 1910 rather than in 1998, the world at large would have been ignorant of his folly. A twenty-five-year-old woman on a covered wagon heading west in 1800 was a different woman than one of the same age living in New York City. In the mid-nineteenth century, the black child in the fields and the black child in the big house saw the world through different eyes.

What you are, what you do, and how you are viewed are largely results of time and place—where you are and when you are there.

Leah Lange Chase was twenty-three years old in 1946 and a new bride. Everything she believed about being a wife had been drummed into her by two sources: the women in her family, most importantly her mother, and the teachings of the Catholic Church. *Your husband is everything. You do everything for your husband. He's first in your life. Whatever he wants or needs is your responsibility to provide.*

And that's exactly what she did. He sat in a chair so she could put his socks on his feet. She polished his shoes. She laid out his clothes for him to put on. Women like her did those things then. It was important if you wanted to be considered a good wife, and Leah would be good; she would be good at everything she did.

Today, she thinks she should have gone to her mother's side when the phone call came telling her that her mother's pneumonia was much worse, but she didn't. "You have a husband and children to take care of," her husband told her. Yes, she did. *When my mother died, I was cooking in that kitchen.*

She was not a voting member of the family corporation that owned the restaurant. While the corporate members met upstairs, she stayed in the kitchen, cooking, often collecting IOUs rather than a paycheck. If the financial situation was a bit snug, her husband's family members were paid first. Leah's mother-in-law never understood Leah's feelings of being excluded. "Well, Leah, you're Dooky's wife. When he dies, his part is yours."

When her father-in-law was in the hospital, Leah bathed him and fed him until he died. She cared for her bedridden mother-in-law, Miss Emily, changing her sheets, ironing her nightgowns and robes, seeing that she was comfortable, and listening as Miss Emily told her, "Now, Leah, this ring is for you. And this one is for Stella, and this one is for Emily . . . when I die." Family jewelry passed from hand to hand with each death: father-in-law, mother-in-law, sister-in-law, and old aunts. Despite what she was told, Leah and her daughters were never in the chain of recipients.

The idea of waiting around for someone to die in order to get something seemed to Leah like vultures waiting to feast on carrion. *You want it? Take it. Take it right now so I can see the happiness in your face when it's yours.*

That's what Leah tells her daughter, who jokes, "I want that painting when you die."

You want it? Take it off the wall right now. Take it.

Leah Chase wanted to build a house for herself, a nice house where she could entertain the members of her very large family. She missed family socialization in the early parts of her married life. Her daughter, Emily, used to rise before dawn and cook breakfast and prepare coffee for her husband and his hunting buddies. It was a warm and happy time. Leah envied her daughter's home life and the camaraderie she shared with her husband.

She thought that once the children were gone she and Dooky would find the easy comfort that often develops in middle-aged couples. Leah is a wise woman. She knew the raging love she had felt for her husband when they were young couldn't continue forever. And she knew the demands of raising their children had taken a toll on the couple's relationship. But she thought now that those two phases had passed, everything would settle down and she and Dooky would chat together, watch television together, and joke with each other, like other couples their age. It didn't happen.

After cooking all day at the restaurant, Leah would be driven home to their house on Dumaine Street. Driving a car was one thing Leah failed to learn. *Didn't want it bad enough, I guess.* She thought Dooky would start coming home and they'd live as a couple again. But Dooky couldn't. He was afraid to leave the restaurant empty and unprotected. Years earlier, when the security guard at the restaurant had died, Dooky moved into the small upstairs apartment at the restaurant that had housed the man. By the time the kids left home, home, to Dooky, was the restaurant . . . and he stayed.

Finally, I stopped going home and I slept there, too. It was too hard. Going home late at night to an empty house, getting up early in the morning to get back to the restaurant. Alone. So I went back. But I can't live that kind of life. I'm going to build myself a house right across the street. I'm going to have to do it by myself.

One can argue that no man and no woman really know each other when they decide to marry. At best, they love each other and they gamble that with hard work, their union will bring the life they desire. What could Leah Lange have been thinking when she married Edgar Chase II, only three months after she met him? Only that she loved him. Leah was caught between two chairs: On one hand, her family worried about her marrying a musician. On the other hand, friends of Dooky's family warned them that Leah would be a bad influence on their son. She was different. She was alone in New Orleans, not living at home with her parents like girls her age were expected to. Her independent behavior raised eyebrows. Leah saw and heard the criticism around her, and although it hurt her, she did her best to ignore it. After all, she had been brought up to know the difference between right and wrong, and she made the right choices. She went to bars with friends to socialize but only because there were no other places to go. She knew some people talked behind her back and thought of her as a "loose" woman. But she wasn't.

I fooled them all. I knew myself. I knew Leah. And I knew what Leah could do and would do. After Dooky and I married, my sister-in-law said, 'Leah, you've changed so much.' I never changed. I was the same. They just didn't know me. They judged me wrong.

Everything about Dooky was new and different; he was nothing like any of her former boyfriends. He knew a lot of people; she loved people. They were both attractive and popular and they were grounded in good *Creole-de-couleur* families. Dooky knew Leah was smart. She was witty. He knew she would be a good wife and, above all, a good mother. And Leah? Getting married was something a girl her age was supposed to do. Dooky was a man ahead of his time and Leah was a woman ahead of hers. It seemed inevitable that they would hook up. Leah knew her own strength. She wasn't afraid to make the commitment and make it work.

He caught me. I was good looking, had a great shape. I was real sharp. But I didn't know too much. Dooky liked me a lot. Everyone was talking about this girl who was so this and so that. They nicknamed me Miss Angel and he won the prize. But I truly loved Dooky; I truly did, and I still love Dooky, crazy as he is. I don't regret any of those days, really. Dooky had a band and he was into Dooky. I was young and I just wanted to be with him, wherever he was. I once went on the road with the band and that was a trip. I did more carrying instruments and lugging things around than you can imagine. I never performed; I just more or less talked. Dooky composed a number for me to sing and he was so upset with me. He said, 'This is as simple as we can make it. You can do it. All you have to do is wing it.' The name of the tune was 'That's the Stuff You Gotta Watch.' Very simple. But simple as it was, I could not do it. So while the melody was playing I'd just go on the stage and talk it. And then I'd answer silly little questions and stuff like that. I just couldn't do the music part. It wasn't me.

When Leah and Dooky married, Leah was still striving—striving to escape poverty, striving to be recognized, striving to BE somebody. Dooky had it all. He WAS somebody: popular, handsome, charming, and, by most standards, wealthy. His father was the only black man in New Orleans who owned a Model T Ford. He composed music. He played the trumpet. He was a teenage bandleader, a star. A local newspaper, the *Louisiana Weekly*, called his orchestra the Pride of New Orleans.

When the Korean War started, Dooky's orchestra suffered. Key musicians shelved their instruments for Uncle Sam. His father became ill and his mother needed him in the family business. His dreams of becoming a great musician disintegrated in the face of duty—duty to his mother and to his wife and young children who

The Dooky Chase Orchestra (Dooky standing in the center)

needed a father at home, not one on the road. Dooky threw in the towel. One can only guess what would have happened in the family had Dooky been able to pursue his dreams in the world of music. But Dooky's ethics were clear and he knew where his responsibility was. He took his place at the restaurant.

Dooky had been interested in music since the age of twelve. He remembers his father whistling a lot and credits his dad with having a great ear. At Craig Elementary School, Dooky wanted to be a clarinet player but ultimately chose the trumpet. He then went to Booker T. Washington High School, known for its outstanding music department and for its teacher, John Henry Wilson, from Alabama State College. At the age of sixteen, he organized an orchestra of sixteen members.

Although the band lasted five years (1945 to 1949), Dooky knew from the beginning this would not be his life's work. Black orchestras had to play in lousy places and musicians' wages were low. Plus, changes were in the air. Small bands were becoming more popular than orchestras, and the war in Asia was on the horizon.

Dooky was good. He played solo trumpet, but if any member of the band had to be out, he could fill in, regardless of the instrument needed. And the members of the Dooky Chase Orchestra were good, too. Benny Powell played the trombone and later played with Count Basie. Big Emory Thompson played the trumpet and later played with Lionel Hampton. Most of the members of Dooky's orchestra, at least those who had the drive and ambition to do so, later worked in or around New York and Chicago with big-name bands.

Dooky's band toured for two summers before breaking up and made the first acetate recording in New Orleans, in a studio on the corner of Dumaine and Rampart Streets. Other musicians in New Orleans talked about not being good enough to play for Dooky Chase. Surely over the years, as he saw former members of his orchestra hit the big time, he must have wondered about what he might have become. But in fact, he had never allowed that to be an issue. He surprised his band members by being the first among them to marry, and he was the youngest member of the band. When it came time to choose between the life of a musician and the life of a family man, Dooky chose family.

Dooky had some of his father's entrepreneurial spirit. Not only was he a successful orchestra leader at the age of sixteen, but before the age of nineteen, he had promoted the first racially integrated concert at the Municipal Auditorium[1]. As a married man, and after leaving the music world, he continued to keep a high community profile for better than a decade. He was active in the social men's group called the Frontier Club.[2] In the fifties, he worked tirelessly with other activists in the black community to register black voters. He met in uptown living rooms with prominent blacks and whites to discuss Civil Rights activities that were beginning to rumble in New Orleans. He was in the Urban League, supported the NAACP, and was on the first board of directors of the Jazz and Heritage Festival. He and Leah sponsored the Dooky Chase Pomo Softball Team composed of postal workers. When Ernest "Dutch" Morial decided to run for mayor of New Orleans, Dooky wrote the first big check. He and Leah attended balls, decked to the nines, Leah always sporting a lavish dress she had concocted herself. She had a flair for dressing and was pretty. They were recognized, appreciated, respected—a prominent couple in the black community of New Orleans. Dooky Chase was considered a social and civic activist. Leah was following her husband.

Then something happened. It wasn't an abrupt thing like getting up one morning and announcing, "Okay, it's my turn." It must have been a gradual thing. Their roles reversed. Leah moved into the limelight and Dooky stepped back. Leah was ambitious. She wanted the restaurant to grow, to be a beautiful place. She wanted the little old ladies in the neighborhood to come and sit in nice surroundings, to enjoy a nice meal, and to be treated nicely. She wanted to share, to give.

Dooky was frugal. He believed you don't spend what you don't have. You can't be pretentious. You must stay low-key. Dooky didn't want to take risks. Leah wasn't afraid of anything.

My marriage is the biggest disappointment of my life. I love Dooky. I just don't understand him. He used to be pretty active. He just bummed out.

In the middle of their life together, these two very different people with contradictory attitudes and behaviors bumped up against each other, but Leah was moving forward. Doggedly, she began planning the expansion of the restaurant. Dooky didn't interfere. His father's po' boy stand of the 1940s was only a memory. Leah became the restaurant and the restaurant became her.

As in most good Catholic families of that era, children came early and often. Emily was born in 1946, Stella in 1947, and Edgar Chase III in 1949. With three babies in tow, Leah waited before having her fourth and last child. In 1953 she gave birth to a third daughter, and she named her Leah.

Now, when my children came—no way—nothing came between me and my children. My job was to move my children, to move them up. I didn't have anything when I was their age, so I was going to see that they were everything I wasn't. I wanted them to be topnotch because that was what I wanted when I was coming up. I wanted it badly. I wanted visibility, and I didn't have it, so I was going to see that my children had it.

Leah wasn't working in the restaurant while the children were small; she was working at Corpus Christi Elementary School. She was a Girl Scout leader, PTA president, and head of school fundraising. When Edgar Chase III, also called Dooky, was five years old, he knew he would be King of Corpus Christi. All it involved was making and selling pies.

Leah recruited her sisters. They stayed up all night making lemon-meringue pies, twenty at a time, then selling them.

Leah's children (left to right): *Young Leah, Emily, Edgar Chase III, and Stella*

Whoever brought in the most money would be king, and little Dooky won, hands down.

I was never frightened as a mother until Dooky was born. Then I worried. My goodness, is this boy going to be able to be a man? When he learned to drive, it scared me. The idea of a male child scared me.

Edgar Chase III doesn't think he was independent until he was twenty-five. "I didn't have to be. My mother and father provided me with everything I could possibly want and need." All of Leah's children are marked by a strong sense of support. They go to their mother for advice, knowing in advance that they'll be listened to and given the best of her good sense. Leah has advised her son on everything from his business dealings to family issues, particularly on how to raise his children. "She raised us; she's there for us. She grew up in a big family with a lot of support, and she has made sure we have the same. Her siblings, all my aunts and uncles, they watch over me as much as she does," says Edgar.

As a college student, Edgar worked in the restaurant at night. He bartended sometimes and he cleaned up. He liked being a janitor because it was a quiet time, unlike the earlier hustle and bustle of the dinner crowd. "When you're cleaning the place, there's nobody there with you. There's a silence. It's just you, the mop, and the floor."

In the fifties, prior to integration, the restaurant was open practically twenty-four hours a day. It would close at four or five in the morning, after the night people from the French Quarter would come by, and open again a few hours later at 10:30. Edgar like being around the night people—musicians and bartenders who mostly worked the clubs in the French Quarter. They were different, more carefree, and lovable.

A certain Mr. Antoine would come in and play music on the jukebox and start dancing and swishing around. Edgar would tell him, "I think you better go home. Your wife is going to be mad."

Mr. Antoine would answer, "That old woman, Dooky? Don't worry about her. I can handle her."

Then Edgar would tell him, "Mr. Antoine, you better get on home. The sun's coming up; it's getting late." Sure enough, the next night, there would be no Mr. Antoine. His wife would have punished him.

Leah saw that all her children got what they wanted: dolls and lace-covered dresses for the girls and baseball equipment for Little Dooky. He was an only son, just one little boy, but he had the catcher's mitt, the face mask, knee pads, chest protector, the first baseman's mitt, the second baseman's mitt, all the gloves for the outfield, lots of balls, and several bats. The joke among the kids was, "Don't strike out Dooky. If he goes home the game is over."

*We started a team, my husband and I . . . in the New Orleans Recreation Department. I didn't want my son to have to be told, well, you play on So-an-So's team. Uh-uh. I'm going to get you a team. You play on this team. So we started the Dooky Chase Team. The kids were thirteen years old. I didn't want kids younger than that because then they weren't really playing ball. They were just playing around. I didn't have the patience for that. I had a good coach, Luke Delpit. I'm talking **good** coach. Those thirteen year olds were really playing ball. They were good. We kept that team about five years, until Dooky was eighteen.*

Kids were happy to play on the Dooky Chase Team. After each game, they'd swagger down to the restaurant and Leah would feed them hamburgers and hot dogs.

Mardi Gras Eskimos (left to right): *Edgar Chase III, Stella, Leah, Leah Chase, and Emily*

Leah liked parties and holidays. Each year for Mardi Gras, she made elaborate costumes for her and the children, all just alike. They were matadors or astronauts or anything requiring painstakingly sewn outfits. When the Chase family stepped out, people grabbed their cameras, delighted to see such a spectacle. That made Leah happy. On Halloween, she costumed the children and set up a huge table full of candy on the neutral ground[3]. Every kid in the neighborhood knew where to find Miss Chase.

I was going to give everything for my children. I sewed dresses for my little girls so they never had to wear the same dress twice. They were always dressed pretty. I would take everything anybody gave me and sew it, underclothes and everything.

Leah didn't stop when her children grew up. When daughter Leah had a concert or other musical appearance, mother Leah filled the stage with flowers. She is forever telling her grandchildren what to do and how to do, but she's still more concerned about her own children than her grandchildren, and she makes sure the grandkids understand. *Don't you dare make my children unhappy. If you do something to make my child unhappy, I'll punch you out.*

I always told my children, you have to give your children the best education you can give them. You have to do for your children. You have to give up your life for your children. When you bring those children in the world, you're responsible.

I kind of depend on my children to make me happy, to do the things I thought my husband would do for me. You want companionship, someone to talk to, to share with. I don't have that. I have four beautiful children, sixteen grandchildren, five healthy great-grandchildren, everything going well, children educated, grandchildren being educated, everything going well, and the thing that you thought, you know . . . the bottom is working well and the top falls off.

You just want to put a niche in life for yourself and for your children. You want to fit them into a . . . society and push them as high as they can go. I go places with my children. I thought I'd be going places with my husband. But I don't. You just have to play those cards like they're dealt.

Joe Louis (second from left), *courtesy "Speed" Lunnon Porter's Photos New Orleans*

CHAPTER FOUR

You Do What
You Have to Do

Faced with difficult options in her life, Leah Chase has nevertheless always responded with the same answer: *You do what you have to do.* It's the belief that raises her out of bed when she's dog-tired, makes her smile at her clients when she's fed up, and attracts her to people whom she reads about, who, when forced to, reach back and give a second effort, more than they were capable of doing initially.

My whole fight in life was to be accepted. When I went to St. Mary's Academy, it was so hard for my mother and father to keep me there, even when the tuition was only ten dollars a month. It was hard. That was a lot of money in those days. Those nuns would make preferences between people who had money and people who didn't have money. Sometimes, there were preferences for people who had lighter skin. One time, I'll never forget, I had on this very pretty pink organdy dress my mother had sewn for me, and she had put little pink and blue ribbons on it, and it had little blue elephant buttons. And I was so happy because the nun said, 'Oh, that's a pretty dress.' She had never said anything at all about anything I had on. They would look at you differently because you were poor. It was awful, really awful. You had to battle all those things.

My Aunt Lucy had to move and I had no place to stay so my mother asked the sisters if I could stay at the school as a boarder. They let me stay there for a couple of months. While I was there, a girl whose aunt was the mother superior of the order was also a student. I was in the convent, and I could iron. I had to go after school and iron all of that girl's blouses, because all of her blouses had to be ironed 'just so,' and I could iron 'just so.' She was a little girl in grammar school and I was in high school. I had to take care of her and iron her blouses. That helped pay my way.

Once, a professor from Xavier, who taught French, came to St. Mary's and I got an award for speaking French. You know those nuns were prejudiced as heck. They were all black. Prejudice can be anywhere. Poor darlin's, I guess they did the best they could. This nun said, 'You know So-and-So should have gotten that award.' Now, I know I knew French better than So-and-So did. She had pretty long hair. I was poor; she wasn't. When you were poor in my day, that was bad news. People looked down on you. So you had to rise above that poverty if you wanted to be anything or if you wanted to feel like a person.

I always think about that and try not to hurt people. But you know what that did to me? It made me fight. It made me battle and I'm always battling. Every time someone tries to knock me down, I battle.

My struggle was to overcome poverty. You know, in the country you can see beautiful rainbows. I'll never forget my mother. . . . After it would rain, my mother would call us: 'Come and see the pretty rainbow.' And I would stand in the yard and look at the rainbow and I would say to myself, 'I know, I know there's a pot of gold at the end of that rainbow.' Wasn't that stupid? And I knew I could walk to it. I used to always wish to walk to the end of the rainbow. Crazy. But you have ambitions and you do what you have to do.

*You had to always be beating things down and you had to do it quietly. You couldn't make noises. Maybe if I'd been young when those '60s people came up, I'd have been right in there with them, because all of my life I had to be quietly beating doors down and not upsetting anybody else and trying to climb, trying to climb all the time. And I don't know if that's good or not. I used to wish at times that I didn't have that disposition. I used to wish at times that I were more like my sisters who would just be satisfied with whatever. I don't know; I was just always **out there**.*

Leah recognizes that she is different from many of her peers. Sometimes that bothers her to the point that she prays to change her ways.

I'm stubborn. I like to do things. I like to move on things. And when I move on things, I'm not going to take anything from anybody. I just want to move all the time. I'm always climbing, always grabbing, but not in a greedy way, because I give everything away. I'll never be rich because I give away more than I can afford to give away. I don't know what makes me climb all the time. I actually prayed that I wouldn't be that way. I cannot be a big fish in a little pond. There's not enough room for me. I'd rather be a little fish paddling like heck in a big pond.

As a young person, the people who attracted me were people with strength who just did things. I liked people who were strong—physically and emotionally strong. And I always admired those who could reach back and get more if they needed it. You have ball players like that. Josh Gibson, who played for the St. Louis Cardinals, was like that.[1] He could go nine innings, and if they'd go into overtime, you'd see him reach back and he could pull that power. Physical strength and stamina always impressed me. You would think you could break him or weaken him but he would always make that second effort. And I try to be like that. I try to reach back for that second effort. That's why I like [U.S. Gen.] George Patton. He was tough, he was determined, he set a goal and he was going to reach that goal at any cost. He slapped a soldier that was 'breaking' on him. Here were all these men sick and injured and maimed and this guy was going to 'wimp' on him? **No.** *If you went to war with George Patton, you went to war. And you better put your tie on. He was meticulous— rough, raw. But that was the nature of his business. I like people with determination who set goals for themselves and can carry them out.*

I always followed Eva Perón. I read everything about her. She picked herself out of the gutter but she couldn't hold on at the height she achieved. Bill Clinton is controversial but I give him credit for hanging in there, hanging tough. I like the way he and his wife hang tough. Not that I admire some things about him. I like people who are what they are, and you know what they are, so you don't have to make any bones about it. I know where he's coming from all the time. And John Glenn, he is unbelievable. To do what he did, to go up in space again at his age, is unbelievable and gutsy. This is **not** *an easy program.*

When I was young, nineteen or twenty, I managed a couple of boxers.

Joe Louis visited St. Mary's Academy when I was a student. He was a gentleman, a very smooth man, very humble, easygoing—just easy, no big thing. In those days, boxers didn't have all that mouth. Either they could box or they couldn't. A couple of young people asked me, 'Would you manage us?' I said, 'Okay.' That wasn't for very long. Local guys, one went off to fight in the U.S. Marines. They were good boxers. I'd try anything one time. I saw that they had the proper equipment, were given the fights they needed, were getting their money—enough of the gate, enough of the purse. That was 1943-44. I liked to position myself where I could meet other people: Beau Jack, world champion, and Bob Montgomery. The fights were held in Coliseum Arena, raggedy old place. There was no good place. Everybody went to the boxing matches. That was the only entertainment on weekends.[2]

Later I worked for a man who had racehorse books. I needed a job and that was a good one. In those days, if you could make ten or fourteen dollars a day, that was good money. So I said, 'I could learn to do that. I could learn to mark that racehorse board. You could hire me.' At that time, there weren't any women doing the things I was trying to do. I was young, good looking, easy to hire. I could catch on and do that. And after I did it, little white girls started getting those jobs, coming in on those racehorse boards. I was there to mark the horse, like 6-2-even: six dollars to win, two dollars to place, even money to come in third or show. And I learned to mark them so the bookies could make money, learned the percentages to mark them. I'd get a report that a horse was running 30-12-8. The bookie isn't going to pay 30. All he's going to pay is 20. So you mark the horse 20.

My life has been like a game of checkers. You put your hand on your checker and you want to go here. But you don't take your hand off, because you see if you make that move you'll lose, so you keep your hand on the checker because you decide to change. So you move in another direction. Then you say, 'Okay, this is the right track.' And you go and go. But you've got to know when to pull out, when to bet, and how to still be a lady and be respectable. And I learned to do that real young. You know, when you're young and you're trying to climb that ladder, you're grabbing on anything you can grab. Then when you find out this is not going to get you anywhere, this is not what you want to be, you let that one go and you get another one.

We're still struggling to try to come up. None of us, to me, should be able to take one road and say, 'I'm going to take this road, because it's a paved road. And it's nice and smooth.' We have to hit the rocky roads, too. And I feel that's what I had to do.

Little did Leah know there was a rocky road before her when she entered the family business: the Dooky Chase Restaurant.

There was almost nobody for me to learn from. When I came to the restaurant in 1946, I came from the French Quarter. Before I got married, I worked for a lady in the Quarter who had a restaurant, the Colonial Restaurant, that served dinners and lobsters and all that stuff. I went to wait tables for her; she taught me everything. And I saw people do things in the kitchen, I saw how they operated, and I loved it. Then she opened up the Coffee Pot and it was a short-order thing, just breakfast and hamburgers and that kind of stuff. I started selling hot lunches over there for her. I did that with another waitress.

When I came to this restaurant, I had to do everything. There was nothing really—nothing. I had to work from scratch. You make a lot of mistakes. First, I made meatballs and spaghetti like I did for Miss Sauveur. Then I said, maybe we should do dinners.

I found that lobster Thermidor wasn't going to work. People said, 'What is this?' They didn't understand at all. So I started stuffing the lobster head with shrimp dressing and broiling the tails and they could deal with that. But I had to wing it. I had to wing it hard. And when I think about it, I don't know how I did it. I don't know. I worked endlessly in here. I'd get through working at night, then I'd take a bucket of water and go to washing the walls and scrubbing the ceiling, doing things, changing things. That's why . . . it's hard for me. I put my heart and soul and my life in here. It's just hard for me to say, 'I quit.'

I used to do everything in here. We just had that little kitchen over there and that shelf where those spoons are, that's where we used to put the tea. Now I'm a tea fanatic. I insist that you boil that water for that tea and put it in there. Don't give me any tea that isn't boiled and steeped. So I went to lift that three gallons of tea up on that shelf, as I did every day, and missed it. Down came the boiling tea, right down my bosom—boiling tea all down me. And besides, I had ulcers. The burn just threw me into one knot. My stomach cringed. I buckled. I wanted to call the doctor. Here comes this girl who was waiting tables who says, 'You got to throw flour on it.' Now I remembered my Aunt Esther who patted her burned foot with filé and a sweet-potato pod and she almost lost that foot.[3] So I say, 'No you don't. Just call the doctor.' When I got to the hospital, Dr. Epps told me the worse thing an ulcer patient can do is get burned. I don't know if it's because of the shock of the pain, but acid drips into the stomach and throws you into a tizzy, and that's what it did. I was in pain—in pain. I was going to the doctor everyday, blisters under those bandages. I was bandaged like a mummy but working in this kitchen everyday. I did not stop working. And I did all that work with these bandages and these blisters. I've just damaged myself all to pieces in this restaurant. Here on my arm, it was cleaning that big grill. Nobody could clean that grill so I did it myself and it burned me to pieces. But you keep going. You put a little powder on your face and you keep going.

Like many couples, Leah and Dooky's differences were less visible in their younger days but became paramount with age.

Dooky thinks he can run a business on nothing. Without spending any money. 'We don't owe anybody anything.' Now did you ever hear of such a stupid thing in your life? At the same time, we don't have anything either. It takes money to make money and you have to move and do what you have to do. The one thing I'm trying to do, and I'm going to do it! I just hope I get this thing off the ground . . . put my house on the corner. I don't think I can restore that building. I think I have to come down with it. I'd put a double shotgun there, something that would be fitting for the neighborhood.[4] Can you imagine the people coming down the street saying, 'Gosh, look at all this in this neighborhood?' The neighbors would be so happy, and they would help me do anything I wanted to do. But to get Dooky to move is something. That's why I say, don't tell me about family business; it is bad news.

"Doing what she has to do" extends beyond the walls of the restaurant.

When Donald Mintz ran against Sidney Barthelemy for mayor, Dutch Morial walked into this restaurant and said, 'Leah, you have to go with Donald. And you have to cochair that campaign with Michael Bagneris.[5]

I said, 'Okay Dutch.' I'm not educated but I can work behind somebody as I did with Dutch. I did a lot of things. That's my way of helping. But Dutch was the one with the brains.

Donald was a protégé of Dutch. He was everything like Morial, but he was white and Jewish. He knew how to get to the people, he knew what to do, he wasn't a dummy either, and he was going to be a good mayor. If Dutch would have lived, Donald would have been mayor.

*But Dutch died. Then, in the next election, Mintz ran again, but this time Dutch's son Marc entered the race. I supported Mintz. And people said, 'Oh you're going to do this against Dutch.' They said all kinds of nasty things. I didn't even choose to tell them why I did it. My mama always said, 'Never explain why you did something. Friends don't need it; enemies won't believe it.' I didn't have to say to Marc, 'Look your daddy told me to support this man. Your daddy told me to do everything I could for this man. I did it. Now he's running again, but it's against you.' Where's my integrity if I had gone with somebody else? I supported him the first time; why wouldn't I support him the second time? If I thought he was good one time, what would make me change this time? You can't do that. And I wasn't about to do that. You just **cannot do** that.*

My daughter, Leah, thinks she taught me a lesson about politics. She thinks she taught me a lesson, poor child, to keep my mouth shut. But I go underground, just change tactics. You just don't come out blabbing all over the place. You just do what you have to do. There is no way in this world, in this day and age, anybody who wants to live in the world and be a part of the world, can say, 'I'm not political'. No way. Some kind of way, in some form or fashion, you become political.

Just do what you have to do. Just take the chance. And that's what that book I Dream a World *was all about. I was so proud to be in there. When I saw those people in there, every last one of them. They just did whatever they had to do.*[6]

Lucky for her family, friends, clients, and indeed, all who know her, Leah has never wavered from her commitment to do what she has had to do. Like anyone, Leah's had moments when she could have easily thrown up her hands and quit, but she never has. At this point in her life, it's probably safe to say she never will.

Leah in her kitchen preparing for a large group

CHAPTER FIVE

Kitchen Ambassador

At 11:00 P.M. on September 9, 1965, Hurricane Betsy was thirty-five miles southwest of New Orleans, slapping the city with winds clocked at one hundred and twenty-five miles per hour. The destruction already done since Betsy hit land was unparalleled in the history of Louisiana. When it was over, Betsy would leave eighty-one people dead and over 17,600 injured. More than 250,000 people would have evacuated their homes and sought safety in storm shelters. Damages from the storm would be estimated at over two billion dollars.[1]

A city sitting below sea level, New Orleans caught the brunt of the hurricane. Seven-foot flood waters swept parts of the city. Large numbers of snakes, seeking high ground, caused the Army Corps of Engineers to issue snakebite kits to all personnel. Dangerous bands of dogs, driven wild by the lack of food and care, threatened the already devastated residents in flooded areas.[2]

Betsy knocked out the city's electricity. Leah Chase's freezers were filled with oysters, catfish, soft-shell crabs, gumbo, and other menu items. Leah made a plan. She contacted the city police and told them: "I'll cook up all this food before it spoils and you help me get it to the folks out there who don't have electricity and are stuck in their homes."

The plan worked. Leah and her assistant fired up the gas stoves, ovens, and deep-fat fryers and started cooking. Every few hours, she would meet a police escort, make her way by foot along the levee of the Mississippi River, and get food to people in the low-lying areas. Ferdinand, one of her employees, was a prime target. *There he was, stuck out there in his house with children to feed and no wife. I had to help him.*

Leah's role was a small part of a much more sophisticated operation. The American Red Cross flew in eleven Army Field Kitchens
to prepare and serve one million meals to disaster victims and
emergency workers.[3] When the storm ended, the city faced the
most colossal collection of garbage, trash, fallen trees, blown-down
signs, and broken glass and roof tops in its history. And Leah's
freezers were empty.

It doesn't take a hurricane to shift Leah into action. Once she
happened upon a man digging in a garbage can on the side of the
road. Leah told her daughter to stop the car: *You don't have to do
that. You don't have to dig in a garbage can to get something to eat. Come
by the restaurant. I'll give you something to eat.* And she did. *I can't
stand that. I can't stand to see people digging in garbage cans for food. If
I can help them, I will. Jesus said to feed the poor and take care of the sick.
I don't know . . . maybe some of those poor people are God, testing me.*

Leah Chase's good will goes beyond need. She's a great believ-
er in taking care of individual wants and desires. She likes to place
all of the restaurant reservations herself, because that way she
knows which clients are seated at which tables, and from the
kitchen, she mentally follows the service. If she serves you once,
she knows your quirks.

When a certain judge comes in, he doesn't order; he simply tells
the waiter to tell Mrs. Chase he's there. *Yes, sir. Okay. I know the
judge wants his catfish and his potato salad on the same plate, and then
he wants one little dish of sweet potatoes on the side. And he likes to tell
whomever he's with, 'She knows exactly what I want.'*

Another preferential client is Colonel Stillman. Col. Richard
Stillman was secretary of the general staff of the United States
Army during World War II and his office was next door to one of
Leah's heroes: Gen. George Smith Patton, Jr. Mutual love, respect,
and admiration for General Patton have made unlikely allies and
good friends of Leah and Colonel Stillman.

What can I fix you today, Colonel Stillman?

"A little broiled fish, just lemon and no seasoning. And just a
green salad. A few steamed veggies. And some bottled water and
a glass of orange juice." Colonel Stillman doesn't need a menu,
much less consults one.

A special target of Leah's generosity is her church, St. Peter

Early days of restaurant—1940s interior (Edgar Chase I seated with his back to the wall)

Claver Catholic Church. Located in the Treme neighborhood, it is the largest black Catholic church in New Orleans. Father Mike Jacques, her priest, knows he can count on her. "I called her at 10:00 A.M. one morning and told her I had twenty-five people for lunch. I had forgotten to call before. No problem. She sent over salad, vegetable, dessert, and po' boys, napkins, plates, forks, knives, everything. If we have a church fair, she cooks all the food for the fair, for four hundred to five hundred people. She cooks it; we pick it up. There's never been a single time I've asked Leah for something that she hasn't delivered. Board meetings, deanery, bishops, guests from out of town. . . . She's never turned me down."

If a group wants a breakfast meeting at the restaurant, Leah is there at 7:00 A.M., by herself, cooking: quail, cheese grits with shrimp, grillades, biscuits, and bacon and sausage.[4] She prepares the same breakfast every Father's Day, just for her extended family. It isn't unusual for forty or fifty kids, grandkids, nieces, nephews, sisters, brothers, and in-laws to show up.

When William Jefferson decided to run for the United States

Congress in 1990, one person he ran against was Leah's son, Edgar Chase III. Jefferson won, but this did not inhibit his regularly seeking out "Mother Chase" to chat and benefit from her advice. They remain friends. In 1992 Congressman Jefferson was on a bus of Clinton-Gore supporters rolling across the South. He called Leah. "I've got a busload of people supporting Bill Clinton and we're not far from New Orleans. We're coming to your place to eat. You set the menu."

Leah does not reserve special treatment for VIPs. Anyone is fair game. People have learned they can depend on her. After an old friend had an operation, Leah cooked food for her and her entire family and sent it over in a cab. She has a mental list of friends to whom she sends food in cabs. She knows what they like and how they like it prepared.

Leah's clients know her so well they feel free not only to order entire takeout dinners from her, but also to tell her how to cook. *'And now, I want you to go get eight bunches of greens and I want you to do like I do. I wash them three or four times. . . . And make my potato salad just like my husband used to do before he died. My daughter and I work hard so we're too tired to do this. We appreciate you doing this but you have to do it exactly like he did it. My husband made the best potato salad in the world. . . . Now, I want the eggplant casserole but don't put any salt in it because you know Mama can't have all that potassi-ISM.'* This request earned "Mama" a new nickname in the kitchen: Miss Potassi-ISM.

There's one lady who comes in here—eats nothing but chicken wings. 'Now, I want my chicken wings broiled. Four chicken wings broiled.' One time she came in: 'No, you know they were not broiled right because they were not brown. You have to brown them.' Okay, lady, we're going to brown them. . . . 'And cook me some squash. But the last time the squash had a little bit too much water. Cook it down a little bit further. And don't put any shrimp in there, I can't have shrimp.' All these special orders. 'I drink nothing but fresh-squeezed orange juice. So when I come, get the oranges.' Has to be squeezed when she comes in. Is that crazy?

Another lady, when she comes in, she has to sit at a certain table. Or she'll reserve a whole room for three people. But if she doesn't reserve the Gold Room, she'll sit only at that particular table, nowhere else. And I have to come out. Doesn't matter if I'm busy. I have to come out and say hello. It'll drive you mad.

I have one lady who will call, 'You know what I like? I like that shrimp

Left to right: *Congressman William Jefferson, Leah Chase, Al Gore, Edgar Chase III*

pasta. And strip that catfish for me.' She'll order weird. 'Send me two dozen stuffed shrimp.' She's not going to eat two dozen stuffed shrimp but that's what she orders. 'And make me that sweet potato I like, you know, with those marshmallows on top?' She doesn't get out of her house. Hasn't been out of her house in I don't know how many years. I send the food over to her with one of the waiters.

You just have to deal with these old people. Right around the corner, poor darling, she died when she was ninety years old. We used to take her dinner to her every day. She loved fried oysters. 'Now don't fry them too hard. You know, yesterday they were too hard.'

They think you belong to them. They'll tell you, 'I feel like I'm in my own house.' Sometimes there will be more people in the kitchen than you can shake a stick at. Eugene used to say, 'Miss Chase could you take the people out this kitchen so we can do our work?'

Man comes in, and before he even sits at his table, he walks back into my kitchen. 'What you got special for me today?' I don't have anything special; could you just order from the menu? But no, he wants me to do something special for him. But I think I've made them like that. They're just spoiled. They know when they come here it's like they're the only people in the world. Aunt Sadie will come in and say, 'You know what I

Former sous-chef, Eugene

want. Give me my gumbo.' She loves gumbo. Not supposed to have it but that's what she orders, every time. And she'll say, 'Fix my fish with that angel-hair pasta.' Or she loves pasta primavera, just with vegetables, so we've named that the Aunt Sadie special.

Until 1984, guests at Dooky Chase's were served in a small dining room that opened through double doors directly onto the street. The atmosphere was homey and tables were limited. An upstairs room was used for private parties, including everything from social groups, like the Original Illinois Club, to political caucuses, like the Southern Christian Leadership Conference.[5]

Then Leah realized a dream, adding an entrance, main dining room, and medium-sized dining room to the existing space. The original small dining room is now the Gold Room and serves small groups. The Victorian Room can serve as many as fifty-five in a private group, and the main dining room is always set for at least ninety individual diners. The famous Upstairs Room, a room that made history, has been relegated to office space.

Leah used her grand opening to good advantage. The World

Dooky Chase Restaurant until the 1950s

Dooky Chase Restaurant after the 1980s renovation

Exposition of 1984 was opening in New Orleans and Leah was keenly interested in its success. She wanted it to showcase New Orleans and the best of all things the city had to offer. One of the pavilions, I've Known Rivers, was in financial trouble.[6] *I said, 'Okay, I go to a lot of openings where you pay.' I called everybody and I said, 'This is what we're going to do. We're going to have this opening and we're going to charge fifty dollars per person, and the money is going to I've Known Rivers.' So I put my little feelers out. Mayor Morial was coming to cut the ribbon. We did the whole kit and caboodle. We gave everything. None of the money came to me. We had this place packed. I put out food like you wouldn't believe. The whole Gold Room was set up as a buffet. We had food. We had music. We had everything. I think we made between eight thousand and ten thousand dollars for I've Known Rivers.*

Special events in the city start Leah's creative juices working and, to quote one of her friends: "It's never done until it's over-done." When the Sugar Bowl hits town, Leah decorates her tables with flags of the opposing teams. She always draws a crowd, and when the fans enter her dining room, she wants them to be happy—ALL of them. *It's a hoot when Ole Miss comes to town, all those Rebel flags on my tables in my restaurant. They always come in droves, some of my best customers. Can you beat that?*

Taking care of the whims and needs of local folks is a Leah Chase specialty. One of her pet projects is the New Orleans Museum of Art, where she is a lifelong member of the board of trustees.

"Miss Chase, one of your *tin-tins* brought you this." Ce, a waiter, has worked for Leah for several years. He walks hunched slightly forward and never too fast. His eyes cover the tables in the dining room in easy sweeps, and he deftly lifts empty plates and glasses, asking the guests if they'd like coffee or dessert. He's a calm presence in a busy place. He hands Leah a bouquet of flowers. She bursts out laughing. *Tin-tin* is a Creole expression for little old lady—sophisticated, retired. The tin-tin in question is one of the many volunteers at the New Orleans Museum of Art. Leah regrets she can't do more for the museum. One thing she CAN do is feed the volunteers. The day before the flowers' arrival, she had sent forty-five chicken lunches to the museum volunteers. They had been delivered before 11:30 in the morning.

Grand opening: (left to right) *Edgard Chase II, Leah Chase, and Mayor Dutch Morial*

Left to right: *Leah Chase, Roger Dickerson (composer), and Antoinette Handy (flutist)*

When Leah is the guest chef on the local WDSU television program called *Alec's Kitchen,* the entire staff at Channel Six knows they're in for a treat. The formula for the program appears simple: the guest chef appears and cooks and the recipes are shown to the viewers. What actually happens is this: the chef arrives with the entire meal precooked and camera ready, plus all the ingredients needed to prepare the same meal on camera. Hours of preparation are necessary for twenty minutes of camera time. The chef must also have all the utensils necessary to prepare the meal, down to the dishtowels and sponges for cleaning up. Leah's spices are premeasured into miniscule containers; her wooden and metal spoons, mixing bowls, blocks of butter, knives, wire whisk, cooking oil . . . everything she will need to cook with is there and organized.

The show ends with the chef and host Alec Gifford eating the meal. Sure enough, the table is set with Leah's tablecloth, napkins, dishes, glasses, knives and forks, down to the salt and pepper shakers and bottle of hot sauce. To get her things to the show, Leah had used three heavy-duty cardboard boxes the size of suitcases, plus five ten-gallon stainless-steel containers. Her daughter's car trunk had been stuffed when Leah arrived at the station at 7:30 A.M. She had been cooking and preparing since 2:00 A.M. The reason? When she appears at Channel Six, she brings enough prepared food to feed the entire studio of over seventy employees. A cameraman remarks, "That's the difference between her and other guest chefs; she feeds us all." Producer Lenora Cannon comments, "It's like working with your mother." People think of her as a mom and her restaurant as their home, and she understands that. It's an image she's cultivated.

A white couple I know from California, he was friendly with my sister, moved here and he gave his girlfriend her engagement ring right in my kitchen. Yes, he did—took it out of his pocket, introduced me to the girl, and gave her that ring right there in my kitchen.

What goes on here some days will drive you crazy. You just wonder. Some days that's what keeps me going. . . . Out of the clear, here comes Orlando. He came here to go to Ochsner because he'd been told he didn't have much time to live.[7] Then Ochsner gave him a clean bill of health. And I said to myself, 'Oh boy, I bet this boy is full of baloney'—but no. He had money and paid for his food. And he came the next night, then he came back Saturday, and last night. So he called me this morning and he said, 'I just think you are so beautiful. Put some lipstick on, you hear? You'll look beautiful all the time.' Wrote me a nice little note. Isn't that strange? You never know. You just never know what's going on in this place.

No, you don't. Sous-chef and niece Cleo greets Leah one afternoon with the question, "What's all these white dresses?" The restaurant had been packed at lunch with family groups and all the ladies were dressed to the nines in white dresses. *A ceremony. An ordination for this woman who was inducted into the ministry. She'll be preaching at a church on Allen Street. That's what the white dresses were for. But that happens here. That still happens. I don't care where you go, you come here after and eat. If at night you go out dancing, you come here after to eat. After graduation, you come to eat here. It's almost like a habit.*

Leah Chase has been the chef in her restaurant for fifty years. In the early days, her sisters gathered in her small kitchen and helped shell crawfish to prepare her recipes; in mid-career, she and her staff of one, her daughter Emily, prepared dinners for six hundred guests of then-mayor of New Orleans Dutch Morial. Now, Leah appears in numerous articles and on local, national, and international television cooking shows, judges cooking contests all over the United States, and writes cookbooks. Her fame draws clients from all over the world to eat her food and just get a glimpse of her, but she's not resting on her laurels. She's in her kitchen, ten to twelve hours a day, still cooking.

Leah Chase has a multinational, multicultural spirit. On St. Patrick's Day, she serves corned beef and cabbage or Irish stew. St. Joseph's Day means pasta primavera. Occasionally, she'll do a Wok and Soul Day. *When the Chinese came here to build the railroads, the slaves were here. So at one time or another, they had to mingle together. They had a rapport with each other because, according to the white man, they were all on the same level—workers. Blacks started liking Chinese food. Chinese restaurants opened up in black neighborhoods.* On Wok and Soul Day, Leah makes "Yakimi," a dish found often in the black community: beef broth with soy sauce, green onions, noodles, and pieces of beef.

One Monday her theme was Russian. Twenty-four Russian entrepreneurs in the restaurant business were seated in the Victorian Room. They were on a tour of restaurants and catering businesses in the United States at the invitation of local Rotary Clubs. Leah prepared a special lunch for them, starting with her own brew of Bloody Marys. *I thought they'd like that. You know, Russians like that vodka.* Her Bloody Mary mix has an extra dash of hot sauce and a surprising touch of fresh dill. The lunch got off to a good start.

Leah, who had been working in the kitchen in black slacks, a black tee shirt, and a Yankees baseball cap, threw on a white smock to welcome the group.

"How's the situation over there for getting help?" she asked.

The translator spoke for them: "It's easy to get help; it's hard to get good help." Leah nodded her head. They understood each other's problems. The Russians had eaten in eight other New Orleans restaurants but they'd not had Creole cuisine.

"My food is *Creole de couleur*," Leah explained. "We add spices, an African touch." She continued, "Monday in New Orleans is red-beans-and-rice day. That's because Monday was always wash day. A lady wouldn't have time to do all the wash and a lot of cooking, so she would just put her red beans and rice on to cook early in the morning and let them go. So one thing you'll eat today is red beans and rice." The Russians were getting a little bit of history.

Leah excused herself from the Russians as they chatted over their drinks, and scurried into the kitchen. She had started cooking that morning at 7:30. At 11:00, she was pouring sugar from a five-pound bag into a stainless-steel dishpan filled with the makings of bread pudding. She dumped a glass of rum into the mix and stirred it with a paddle. Leaving the dishpan on a stool, she opened the oven and set an already buttered stainless-steel baking pan on the oven door. Lifting the dishpan, she emptied the fifteen or so pounds of batter into the baking pan and slid it into the oven. She didn't look at the clock, didn't set a timer, and hadn't measured a single ingredient.

The Russians ate. A waiter skidded into the kitchen and barked, "More bread." Leah grabbed handfuls of buttered morsels and flipped them into the cavernous toaster oven. Her sous-chef, Cleo, tossed salad in a bowl easily the size of a number-two washtub. Catfish strips fried in the deep-fat fryer. With lightning speed, Leah and Cleo set the salad plates on huge brown trays, filled them, and added the garnish of flash-fried oysters, four to a plate. Two waiters raised the trays over their heads and whisked the salads to the waiting Russians. Leah ladled up rich, red-brown gumbo. The two waiters came and went. Cleo grabbed the hose on the deep dishwashing basin and rinsed dirty dishes. Leah's earlier question to the Russians made a lot of sense: How's the situation over there for getting help?

Back in the Victorian Room, the noise level of spoken Russian and laughter drowned out the piped-in stereo music. Salad plates were removed and bowls of steaming gumbo were set in their place. The waiters laid out a buffet of macaroni and cheese, spicy green beans, jambalaya, red beans and rice, and Creole chicken. As the Russians lined up to fill their plates at the buffet, a waiter slipped in and laid platters of deep-fried catfish strips and tartar sauce on the tables. It was a *groan* meal.

Leah walked in. She stood quietly at the door and watched her guests, smiling. Suddenly, one guest spied her and started applauding. Everyone stood and applauded. Leah smiled broadly.

"Is it okay?"

The Russians burst into exclamations of just how okay it really was. They raised their glasses, and in a verbal language she didn't understand but a body language she knows by heart, they toasted Leah Chase.

CHICKEN CREOLE

6 5-oz. boneless and
   skinless chicken breasts
1 tbsp. salt
½ tsp. white pepper
¼ cup vegetable oil
1 cup onions, chopped
½ cup green peppers,
   chopped
2 cups whole tomatoes
   with liquid

2 cups water
2 cloves garlic, mashed
   and chopped
½ tsp. ground thyme (or 2
   sprigs fresh)
¼ tsp. cayenne pepper
12 small whole okra
1 lb. shrimp, peeled and
   deveined
1 tbsp. parsley, chopped

Season chicken with 1 teaspoon salt and the white pepper. In large skillet or chicken fryer, heat the vegetable oil. Place seasoned chicken in hot oil, turning as it cooks (about 6 minutes). Lower heat. Remove chicken and set aside.

Sauté onions in skillet until they are clear. Add the green peppers; stir and cook for 3 or 4 minutes. Add whole tomatoes, mashing them as you stir them into the onion mixture. Add water, garlic, thyme, cayenne pepper and remaining salt. Let sauce cook on high heat for 4 minutes.

Lower heat; return chicken to sauce. Add okra and cook for 10 minutes until okra are just tender. Add shrimp; let cook until shrimp turn pink (about 5 minutes). Add parsley. Serve over buttered rice. Yield: 6 servings.

At 3:30 on another afternoon, a man with a television camera resting on his shoulder made his way around the dining room taking shots of the art on the dining-room walls. Here, a Jacob Lawrence. There, an Elizabeth Catlett.[8] Alone at a corner table sat a man reading a new biography of Lord Byron. He was Loyd Grossman, host of two television programs: *Master Chef* for the BBC and *Through the Keyhole* for ITV. Two men were setting up lights around one table at the end of the dining room. The master chef on this day was Leah Chase; Grossman had interviewed her before. No stranger to television cook shows, Leah has been on the air in Germany, England, and Italy, as well as Japan. *Funniest thing you ever saw. This big group of Japanese came in here one time to eat my gumbo. They'd seen me on television in Japan.*

Leah had abandoned her white chef's chemise for a shocking pink one. "At my age, I need more color in my life," she stated as she and Grossman sat down at a table. She appeared tense.

"Just pretend the cameras aren't here," counseled Grossman.

"I don't pretend so well," she answered.

A waiter set down bowls of steaming gumbo and Grossman and Leah tasted the thick, hot soup. The cameras rolled. "Umm," said Grossman, motioning to the dishes on the table. "Is this soul food or Creole food?"

"Creole," Leah said. "Creole food has lots of meat, the highest quality. When you use ham, you use thick, lean ham. You use the best cuts of veal. A good Creole breakfast would have grits and breakfast shrimp with braised quail." Grossman learned that Creole cuisine is as much about quality, quantity, and variety as it is about spices.

Grossman asked if New Orleans had gained the reputation of being a food city as early as 1946, when the Chase family first set up shop. Leah didn't hesitate: "We don't eat to live, we live to eat in New Orleans." She explained that historically blacks didn't eat out except for simple meals of sandwiches and gumbo. When Dooky Chase's opened in 1946, it was a po'-boy stand where one could also buy lottery tickets. At that time, the proprietor's take on lottery tickets was twenty-five cents on the dollar. It was good business, and it paved the way for the restaurant.

Grossman leaned back in his chair. He looked at the camera and said a few words. The cameraman backed off and the lights dimmed.

"Are we finished?" Leah asked. This had been fun and interesting, but she had other things to do.

The International Association of Cardiologists was meeting in New Orleans and twenty-five Dutch cardiologists would be in the Gold Room for dinner. The Dutch doctors know and love Leah. They count on eating with her whenever their annual meetings are in New Orleans and call from Holland well in advance to reserve a private room. Leah laughs when she talks about their menu. *I keep telling them I'm not sure all these fried oysters and things are good for them, but they keep coming back.* She always suggests "heart-conscious" foods, but they turn that down. *They like **fried**. The more the better. But I suppose this is the only time of year they eat like that, you know. Those doctors, they're good people. They do what they have to do.*

One of Leah's favorite regular groups at the restaurant is the Elder Hostel Study-Tour Group, headquartered in Boston.[9] Some of the restaurant staff have playfully renamed the group the Hostile Elders. The group loves her cooking, but what they love most is meeting Leah.

"How'd **you** get to be a senior citizen, friend?" she asked one dark-haired member of the group. She continued, "One day I'm going to become a senior citizen, but so far, it's not working out for me. I could make a fortune sitting at home, watching the soaps, and taking in washing, she jokes. I'm way ahead of sixty-five, but I'm enjoying what I do. I enjoy meeting people every day."

The senior citizens took their places at the tables and prepared for a Creole feast. The wind was blowing from the north. *When it blows from the north, it's time for vegetable soup, so that's what you're getting.* What Leah didn't tell them was that the soup would be accompanied by stuffed chicken breasts, stewed okra and tomatoes, the ever-abundant platters of fried catfish and oysters, mixed salad, toasted French bread, and pecan pie.

Before leaving the group to retake control of her kitchen, she told them: "New Orleans has no industry. YOU are our industry. We love you. We want you to enjoy yourself. We'll roll out the red carpet for you. We want you to have a good time. And we don't want you to go home with a penny in your pocket."

Leah Chase with Julia Child

They roared with laughter. They loved her. Leah Chase had just delivered one more group into the arms of the city of New Orleans.

The Dooky Chase Restaurant has been fashioned in Leah Chase's image, making it the most unusual major restaurant in New Orleans. Ray Charles understood its uniqueness and immortalized it in his song, "Early in the Morning Blues": "I went to Dooky Chase/to get me something to eat./The waitress looked at me and said/'Ray, you sure look beat.'/Now it's early in the morning/And I ain't got nothing but the blues."

To the rhetorical question "Would Leah Chase be the same Leah Chase in a city other than New Orleans?", local television news anchor Angela Hill turned the question on its head: "Would New Orleans be the same New Orleans without Leah Chase? I don't think so."

Leah Chase and Jesse Jackson

CHAPTER SIX

Just Feeding Our Clients

Members of the all-white New Orleans Police Department gathered around the doors of the Dooky Chase Restaurant.

"What's going on in there?" they demanded.

Dooky, Leah's husband, pulled himself up to his full five-feet eight-inch height and stared them down. "This is a restaurant. We're just feeding our clients."

Feeding their clients, indeed. Leah and her assistant, Vergie Castle, were inside feeding a revolution. It was 1961.

The Civil Rights fight forced blacks of all colors to forge together, with Creoles being considered among some as the more radical of the group. Because of its Creole population, New Orleans was destined for a unique role in the fight for black citizens' equal rights. The Creole presence is largely given credit for the relatively peaceful integration of streetcars, buses, and schools that occurred in the 1960s. Blacks and whites in New Orleans shared an intimacy not found in other Southern cities. Homer Plessy was a New Orleanian and a Creole.[1] The first black mayor of New Orleans was Ernest N. Morial, a Creole. As early as 1860, Texas had three hundred and fifty-five free people of color, Mississippi had seven hundred and fifty-three, Arkansas had one hundred and fourteen, and Louisiana had eighteen thousand six hundred and forty-seven.[2] The New Orleans Creole society revolved around a number of "social" clubs. These were largely men's clubs operating for the improvement of black schools and public facilities. They were grooming grounds for leadership and they kept people interested and concerned about their community. It was only natural that leaders in these Creole social groups became leaders in the

Civil Rights movement. Arnold Hirsch, a recognized scholar on the subject of New Orleans' Creoles, noted that Ernest Morial was not simply New Orleans' first black mayor but probably the last of the radical Creoles.

The laws in Louisiana in 1961 regarding race prohibited "the sponsoring, arranging, participating in or permitting on the premises any social functions, entertainment, athletic training, games, and other activities involving social and personal contacts in which participants are members of the white and Negro races."[3] Municipal ordinances or commission regulations prohibited interracial contact in public. Ordinance 828 M.C.S., passed by the City Council of New Orleans in 1959, stated: " It shall be unlawful for any of the beverages herein defined as retail, for consumption on the premises, under the same roof, to both whites and Negroes unless the space where such whites and Negroes are served is divided by a solid partition from the floor to the ceiling without any opening therein." So strict were the laws that Tulane University was forced to cancel a Dizzy Gillespie concert. The university authorities learned that Gillespie's piano player was white.[4]

Clearly, the people in the upstairs dining room at the Dooky Chase Restaurant were breaking the law, but Dooky and Leah Chase had made a conscientious decision. The brave people bent on righting one of America's worst wrongs had to eat. Black and white, locals and out-of-towners, in fact, out-of-staters, old and young were meeting, eating, and organizing. It was time for federal Civil Rights legislation to move from the page to the street.

As early as 1954, the NAACP had won the famous case, *Brown vs. Board of Education of Topeka*, where, in a unanimous decision, the Supreme Court ruled that the doctrine of "separate but equal" had no place in the field of public education. In fact, a New Orleans' case, *Bush vs. Orleans Parish School Board*, was upheld with the same decision.[5] The continued segregation of New Orleans' public schools until 1961 was only one example of how little an impact federal legislation and judicial decisions had on local communities.

Leah Chase was a civic observer with strong opinions and a desire to make her city a better place for all of its people. Although her priority was raising her children during the 1940s and 1950s, she was better versed than many on Civil Rights action taking place on the national level. Lester Granger, chairman of the

Edgar Chase II (left), *Dizzy Gillespie* (center), *and Leah* (right)

National Urban League for several years during the early '40s, was a good friend of Pres. Franklin Roosevelt.[6] When Granger came to the restaurant, he and Leah would huddle in a corner and discuss at length all that was going on. Granger claimed that Roosevelt wanted to appoint him to his cabinet but Granger had other ideas. He told Roosevelt, "If you want to do something for me, integrate the military." And although Truman is given credit for integrating the armed forces in 1948, Leah still believes the action was already in the pipeline because of Granger's relationship to Roosevelt.

Most white people had ignored Civil Rights laws and the plights of black Americans without having to confront the reality of what was happening, but the publicity that came from television broadcasts in the 1950s brought the issues right into the living rooms of average Americans. Medgar Evers, director of the NAACP in Mississippi, was gunned down in his own driveway in 1963. The same year, Sheriff "Bull" Connor commanded Birmingham, Alabama, police to attack nonviolent Civil Rights demonstrators, some of whom were children, with vicious dogs, fire hoses, and cattle prods. Four black girls were killed when angry white men bombed Birmingham's Sixteenth Street Baptist Church. All Americans were forced to come face to face with the harsh and inhuman treatment black Americans were enduring.[7]

Beginning in the 1950s, leaders of the Civil Rights movement passed through Leah's doors, ate at her tables, and planned the demise of a Southern monolith—racial segregation. Martin Luther King, Jr., came to New Orleans to launch the Southern Christian Leadership Conference.[8] James Farmer, national leader of CORE (Congress of Racial Equality) and Thurgood Marshall, counsel to the NAACP Defense Fund, met with active members of the local NAACP, such as Ernest "Dutch" Morial and Leontine Goins Luke.

Dr. James Dombrowski, a white man and staff director of the Highlander Folk School, an interracial institution he helped start in 1932, came to town to help. He never left.

I can see him now—Jim, Virginia Durr, all those people from the Highlander School. I used to enjoy them, just talking to them, and they'd all come to eat. Those were fun days.[9]

The Highlander School figured heavily in labor activities and black voting efforts. Among the many people who attended Highlander to learn the skills of protest was Rosa Parks.[10] The Dooky Chase Restaurant was no stranger to Highlander representatives. It was in the restaurant's upper room that they organized the first workers' union at Godchaux Sugar Refinery.[11]

Inspired by the successful boycott of white merchants on Dryades Street, several black students organized a New Orleans chapter of the CORE in 1960.[12] Young activists, such as Oretha Castle, Jerome Smith, and Rudy Lombard, rubbed shoulders and shared ideas with local black civic leaders, such as the Rev. A. L. Davis; Revius O. Ortique, judge; and Lolis Elie.[13] When James Baldwin published *The Fire Next Time*, he visited the CORE chapter in New Orleans for a fundraiser.

Every time James Baldwin came to New Orleans, he came to the restaurant. He was always there with a big hug for me. He was that kind of person, just a lovely little man, short in stature . . . a gentle, kind, nice man.

The white community had its own integrationists: Rosa Freeman Keller, Moon Landrieu, and others. While the Uptown whites held meetings in their living rooms, others met in Leah's upstairs dining room. Eating in the upstairs room of the Dooky

Chase Restaurant, as many as sixty people, blacks and whites, crammed into the space that could comfortably seat thirty. *It was like a sardine can. And climbing those stairs, trying to serve everybody, that was a trip.* They discussed, listened, debated, and set strategy—all over Leah Chase's cooking. A local movement was underfoot.

When the Friends of the Amistad Research Center—one of the largest archives in the nation, specializing in the history of African-Americans—honored Leah Chase, Revius O. Ortique, Jr., retired associate justice, remarked in a letter of appreciation in June 2001:

> "You and Edgar, Jr., and your late mother-in-law, contributed so much to the changes that have occurred in the lives of hundreds of thousands—perhaps millions! Some of whom may never have heard of you, nor of your family! But you affected their lives—and their way of living. The vast majority of them never knew about 'the room-in-the-back, upstairs.' . . . The 'room-in-the-back, upstairs' was the place where we, lawyers, gathered—most often—to challenge each other to do more—to agree on a strategy that would change others—who were hell bent on maintaining the status quo. Most importantly, in nurturing others who demanded change! . . . It never occurred to you to be concerned that we were not able to rent the premises, or even pay for the 'refreshments' you provided. You never asked—we never offered. But some of the most effective legal actions emanated from that 'room-at-the-back, upstairs.' The late Judge Lionel R. Collins and I developed much of the legal metabolism, which became the federal attack on employment discrimination, in the landmark case of *Lewis v. Celotex,* in that "room"!

It was no secret to the local police that when this unique mix of folks wanted to eat and meet, there was only one place in town where that could happen. But as Freedom Rider Rudy Lombard said, "It was as though God threw a protective ring around the restaurant. Nobody ever bothered us there." And why did the police watch but not touch? Jerome Smith, another Freedom Rider, has his opinion: "This was no ordinary place. They [the police] had to be careful how they handled it. You have to remember that everyone in the world in the black community who was somebody had come through those doors. It wasn't just the ragtag activist like myself. I think in some way the powers that be had to be careful."

True, but there was the time somebody drove by and tossed a pipe bomb at the restaurant. The bomb partially exploded and rolled across the sidewalk, down the curb, and under the car of one of the customers eating inside. No one was hurt, and when Leah went to see what the fuss was about, a policeman told her to just go back to her kitchen. Although not much damage was done, a fragment of the bomb was lodged in the wall of the bar, and the message was clear.

Meetings and meals at the Dooky Chase Restaurant were the precursors of peaceful sit-ins at New Orleans' soda fountains and drugstores, peaceful demonstrations on city hall steps, and participation in the Freedom Rides, which began in May 1961. Integrated bus rides from Washington, D.C., through the South to New Orleans would test the Supreme Court's *Boynton* decision, which banned discrimination on interstate carriers. Traveling on Trailways and Greyhound buses, blacks would no longer accept being turned away from restaurants and restrooms along the interstate highways. Many of the riders paid a high price for freedom: days and nights in jails far from home and smuggled getaways wrapped in rugs or blankets in hearses and the trunks of cars, careening down narrow highways sometimes in torrential thunderstorms. More than one Freedom Rider wondered if he or she wouldn't die, not only from demonstrating, but also from fleeing with the help of his or her own collaborators.

To the people fighting the battle for civil rights, Leah Chase was more than the owner of a restaurant. Freedom Riders could arrive at her door dirty, bandaged and tired, and she'd nevertheless send them to get a bath and clean up before she'd serve them. "Like a mother would do," former Freedom Rider Jerome Smith reflected.

They would show up sometimes like the dirty dozens. I'd say, 'Nah, no.' And they'd say, 'You mean we just got out of jail and you . . .' 'I mean, I'm not serving you like that.' They'd go by Vergie's (assistant chef and Oretha Castle's mother) *around the corner and take a bath and come back. They'd come here nice and clean. And they'd eat and talk about their next move. Oretha would have that floor. She was tough. She was really good . . . and smart, too.*

As Vergie's home was home to one of the movement's leaders, Leah lived the revolution through Vergie's eyes. With two daughters on the front lines, Vergie had to have worried.

But she supported them. She had more courage than I did. I don't know if I could have stood by with that faith and let my children go out and submit themselves to so much danger every day. The police watched her house all the time. It had to have been miserable for her sometimes, to see her daughters thrown in jail. But she did everything she could do to support them. Sometimes I didn't like it. Sometimes I didn't understand it. I didn't like the way they were going at things. I didn't like having to hate anybody or having anybody hate me. But then, you learn sometimes [that] you do what you have to do. Sometimes you have to upset things to make them go right, then you go back and fix them. But when it's happening, it's frightening to you.

Yet New Orleans achieved something other Southern cities, such as Birmingham, Alabama, and Jackson, Mississippi, did not. It integrated without the violent disruption caused by aggressive outsiders.

Because we knew one another better. You had whites who were really reliable people, like Rosa Keller and the Sterns, and those people were looked up to in the city. They had the money. They were supporting the whole city, so nobody was going to buck against that. You're not going to cut off the hand that feeds you. No matter what he's doing. If he's doing for blacks, you just put up with that stuff. Anyway, a lot of people knew one another, so it went pretty good.

Opening her doors to mixed-race meetings was not Leah Chase's only involvement in such issues. Another radical movement was underfoot during this period. Led by the tenacious and ideological Virginia Collins, a group that believed American blacks were "a nation in captivity" began meeting upstairs at the restaurant. Collins, born in Plaquemines Parish, Louisiana, had grown up in a radical family and became active in the Southern Conference Educational Fund. Her father was supportive of the idea of black nationalism but believed that "Africa is wherever Africans are." Collins fostered her father's beliefs with the Republic of New Africa, a nationalist group that wanted to gain a territorial homeland in the Southern states, where the black population was concentrated. While Collins herself never came to lead a meeting of the group at the restaurant, one of her "lieutenants" did.

There was this one young man, Rashid. When he came to book his party he said, 'I want to have a meeting of the RNA.' So I said, 'Wait a minute. Sit down. Take that chip off your shoulder and sit down. Let's talk.' So we sat down. 'Okay, you can have a meeting; that's no problem. As long as you abide by my rules, you can have the meeting. You don't cause any ruckus. You don't get loud and noisy. You sit down and eat like you're supposed to eat.' Well, they did. And the police came outside and they watched them. They were very orderly. They had their meeting upstairs then went on.

As New Orleans was a microcosm of movements developing all over the country, it was only a matter of time before the black Muslims made their way to Leah's doors. *We had their meetings and banquets when they were first starting. I didn't have a problem with that. Whatever they thought was their own business. I disagreed with them and I told them so. But I cooked for them. Had to buy a certain little fish from them—whiting—cook it, and feed it back to them. But they were neatly collared and wore ties—a clean group. I'd read the newspaper to see what they thought. As long as they abided by the rules, it wasn't a problem to me. But then one time, in [the] paper, they had an ad showing a man with rats coming out of his mouth. It was supposed to depict pork eaters. Uh-uh, I stopped right there. I eat pork. I'm not going to have people in my restaurant who think people who eat pork have rats coming out of their mouths. Uh-uh.*

The year 1961 was a pivotal year for New Orleans. One of the most daring decisions taken was that of the black community to boycott Mardi Gras. Led by Dr. Leonard Burns, president of the United Clubs, Inc., black New Orleans adopted a "stay-at-home" policy for the Mardi Gras parades. They decided it was wrong to party in New Orleans while their brothers boycotted and marched in Montgomery. Instead, black groups in the city would send money to the NAACP Legal Fund to defend the people fighting so hard for the "movement."[14]

More than one hundred black Carnival clubs blacked out their 1961 Mardi Gras balls. Tuxedo rental businesses in the city slumped. Taverns and restaurants closed down. And although Zulu, the only black Carnival krewe, decided to march, it did so under heavy criticism from the black community, who accused the group of "selling out" to Mayor DeLesseps "Chep" Morrison. Its parade, whose route traditionally took several hours to complete, was over in four hours. There was no traditional "second line."[15]

The accompanying Eureka Jazz Marching Band played half-heart-edly. The spectators were sparse, and white.

Taking the krewe to task for its refusal to support the blackout, the *Louisiana Weekly*, a local black-owned and operated periodical since the early 1900s, stated ominously: "The Zulu parade got off to a bad start. One of the city's heaviest river fogs settled over the Mississippi River water front area. Three white photographers supposedly attempting to follow the 'royal barge' in a small craft overturned and only one was rescued. At press time a search was still on for the other two (presumable) bodies."[16]

While the Mardi Gras blackout was a momentous movement within the black community and an unparalleled stand for princi-ple, black-owned businesses, such as restaurants and taverns, took a big financial hit. In a party town like New Orleans, the biggest party of all is Mardi Gras, and when people party, they congregate in restaurants and taverns. Leah and Dooky never even blinked. They shut their doors and encouraged their colleagues to do the same. Of all the restaurant and tavern owners in New Orleans, no single one garnered the level of respect the Chases held in the com-munity. Had they not joined, and joined early, the movement could have flopped.

Leah and her restaurant figured heavily in other important civic issues. The restaurant became a meeting place for those involved in a voter-registration drive for blacks in 1961. They were largely influenced by a young dynamic black attorney, Ernest "Dutch" Morial. At an inaugural meeting of the Louisiana League of Good Government, held at his house, he announced to the women assembled, "Ladies, if you do what I am suggesting to you this evening, in twelve to fifteen years, you will have a black mayor."

A number of black civic leaders and organizations joined the drive. The Bunch Club, meeting upstairs at the Dooky Chase Restaurant and planning strategies, was one of the more popular social groups involved.[17] Leah's husband, Dooky, hosted their meetings and was passionately interested in their activities. He joined other leaders of the black community, meeting at the home of then-mayor Morrison. They discussed how to raise interest in the people in the black community, as a lack of interest among the very people they hoped to help was their major obstacle. The unified

Center: *Tina Bowman (Catholic nun and Civil Rights activist whose life was recorded in a documentary film made by Harry Belafonte)*

Left to right: *Edgar "Dooky" Chase II; Dooky's sister; James Holtry, Civil Rights activist; Mayor "Chep" Morrison; and Miss Emily, Leah's mother-in-law*

Leah with Jessica Harris (right) *and "Boo"* (left), *who supplies her with filé*

efforts of members of groups such as the Louisiana League of Good Government and social clubs like the Bunch Club paid off. In 1978 Dutch Morial became New Orleans' first black mayor.

Some restaurants are merely restaurants. One goes, sits, orders, eats, enjoys, pays the bill, and returns home. Through the years, Leah Chase has cooked for clients and she has cooked for movements. Her restaurant is more than a restaurant; it's an institution. The average restaurant critic is misplaced here. To effectively critique the Dooky Chase Restaurant, one should know about food, history, human relationships, formal and informal politics, art, good manners, and social justice, just for starters. Indeed, to just sit in the dining room, silently, one can almost feel the walls talk, and they have much to say. Jerome Smith sums it up:

"I never did really see it as a restaurant. I saw it as an extension of a house, like my grandmother's or my aunt's. 'Don't come in here like that boy; tighten yourself up.' They didn't want us taking food outside to eat; they wanted us to sit down at the table and to show a certain respect for the table. I always thought she cared for us so much. She gave us special attention. We knew that she knew we were paying some great dues and she wanted us to enjoy that moment as special, not just to run by the window and grab a sandwich. . . . Once, after a campaign, when we got back to New Orleans, the restaurant was our first stop. There she was with this big smile. I forgot what I had just been through. There were police and state troopers going house to house looking for us on Jackson University campus, and there she was with that big smile. All the other stuff we'd been through was erased."

CHAPTER SEVEN

I Just Pray and Keep Going

Marcus Samuelsson is thirty years old and Leah's friend. Born in Ethiopia and later adopted by Swedish parents, he is the chef of the five-star Scandinavian restaurant, Aquavit, in New York City.

I tell Marcus: I know you don't believe in prayer. Young people like you don't believe much in prayer. But I'm going to tell you, I pray for you every day. I pray for you because I want you to succeed in everything you do. You're an exceptional person and I love people like you. When I tell you about prayer, I don't mean you have to get on your knees every day. Good if you do, but you don't have to. You can offer up your work. That can be a prayer. You can say, 'Well, I'll work this dish extra hard,' and that can be like a prayer.

She means every word she says. *I could not function in my life if I did not pray every day before I started. Every morning I pray, 'Oh Lord, just get me through this day.' Sometimes I say, 'I've prayed; it's up to you.' Or I say, 'Oh God, you just have to take care of me,' and then I go. My niece, Cleo, says, 'God's gonna get pretty well tired of you every day, you coming to him with the same thing every day.' And I say, 'Well, I hope not, because that's the only way I can make it.' When I go to bed, I say, 'Thank you for this day.' And I get up the next day and I say, 'I'm going again, Lord . . .'*

When you pray, do you hear what you're praying? Thy will be done? Well that's what it is. You just let God's will be done, whatever it is. And I do. Sometimes, it's just that strength that takes me through the day. You pray every day and after you pray, you say, 'Well God, I can't do anything more. I can't sit here and pray all day.' You can't do that. You have to work.

Prayer is nothing new for Leah Chase. *In my day, you were poor, you knew you were poor, but your whole aim was to get out of that poverty. In the WPA days, we were so stupid we didn't know **who** was coming to visit* *us, but I suppose it was the social workers.[1] And they would come to see our status. 'Are you working? Trying to work?' So my daddy would say, 'Oh no, we can't have this. We have to work. We have to work.' So we'd pray every night that the shipyard would have work so my daddy could work. We wanted to get off this thing, having these people breathing down our backs.*

Old habits die hard. No matter how tired she is at the end of the day, or how late it is, Leah kneels down and says her rosary.

Over the years, she's had plenty of occasions to test her faith, to rely on prayer. Her first-born child and heir apparent, Emily, was told by her doctor that she should not have any more babies. She'd already had seven children but, at the age of forty-two, became pregnant with her eighth child, a boy. On the evening of March 22, 1990, Emily told her husband good night. She was tired, and she was going to bed. That day had been like any other day. She and her mother had been hard at work in the restaurant, and after work, Emily had made a couple of stops to drop off food to friends in need. Her fatigue proved to be beginning labor. Nathan, already overdue, was born with severe brain damage due to oxygen deprivation caused by an amniotic embolus. Emily died in childbirth. Little Nate died eight months later.

What flashes before your eyes when you hear your child is dead . . . I thought of Rose Kennedy, how she lost all those children.

Dooky told her to wait, not to open the restaurant right away. She opened it. Meetings had been scheduled, commitments had been made, and things had to be done. Leah marched on.

Only weeks after Emily's death, then-talk-show host Angela Hill met Leah for a show that had been scheduled months before and saw the devastation in Leah's face. Emily was dead. Emily's seven children had no mother. And yet, there was Leah, ready to do what she had to do.

When Leah went to check her makeup, Hill asked Leah's son, Edgar, "How does she do it?"

He shrugged, "That's my mother."

Hill reflected, "Nobody can describe whatever it is inside her that makes her get up every day and do the wonderful things she does. Nobody can put it into words."

Leah's daughter, Stella, can: "What got her through Emily's

Emily Chase Haydel, courtesy R. A. Ralph, New Orleans

death was faith and prayer. It's prayer that gets her through every day."

Stella's opinion is nothing to be taken lightly. She has shared her mother's deep faith in a very personal way. Stella clearly remembers telling her older sister, Emily, that she thought she might enter the convent and become a nun. She was reflecting on a talk she had heard during Vocation Week at her Catholic high school. When her sister answered that she thought *she* might enter, too, Stella was indignant. "Oh no," she answered. "They said one out of every *three* girls, so I think *I'll* be the one to go." She began preparing to enter a convent.

Leah accepted her daughter's decision, but Dooky, knowing his daughter would have to leave home and live in Carmel Heights, Pennsylvania, was less enthusiastic. He hated the thought of his daughter being so far from home.

Leah worried. *It really was like losing her. She was losing her freedom. She wouldn't be able to come home when she wanted to. She wouldn't be able to write or call when she wanted to. It was different then than it is today. She would literally be gone.*

Nevertheless, Stella enrolled in the Convent of the Sisters of the Blessed Sacrament and her mother accompanied her there on the train. Stella was happy to have her mother all to herself on the long train trip. Convinced that she had been called by God to fill her vocation, Stella thought they were sharing a spiritual bond that surpassed the relationship of mother and daughter. She felt swaddled in her mother's love and support, and that felt reassuringly good to the seventeen-year-old.

Of course, I was pleased Stella had chosen to give her life to God's work, but I cried all the way to Philadelphia and all the way home. But then, that was that—nothing I could do about it.

Friends and family had questioned Stella heavily, because, after all, she had never been a holier-than-thou kind of girl. She had boyfriends, and although she did the things she was supposed to do—pray, go to church, help the sisters in her parish—she wasn't considered pious. But her mind was made up. She only wavered when it came time to tell her mother goodbye and she asked herself what in the world she was doing to herself, leaving her mother. But the sisters in the convent told her that was normal; it was homesickness and it would pass. And it did.

After four years, and having completed her first vows, Stella began to doubt her calling. As the doubts grew, she sought counseling, particularly from a friend of the family, Bishop Harold Perry. Finally, after much prayer and counseling, she decided to go home. Her father was delighted. He was happy to have his daughter back home. Her mother was disappointed, worried that her daughter had given up. Once again, it was time for Leah to call upon her faith. She went to see her priest and, reassured by him that not everyone who goes into the convent really has the vocation, accepted that her daughter had done nothing wrong or disappointing to God. After all, Stella had not yet taken her final vows. Had that been the case, Leah would have been devastated.

Leah's prayers and faith have sustained her through other painful times. When she took the unpopular stance of supporting Donald Mintz over Marc Morial in the mayoral election of 1990, people sent her vicious and ugly anonymous letters and faxes. Some would call her on the phone, say something nasty, then hang up. For months, her restaurant was virtually boycotted by the city powers that be. She held fast, not bothering to explain her action to the community at large. She knew she had done the right thing.

She worked untiringly for Flint-Goodridge and other associations in the black community, but wasn't good enough to be invited to join LINKS.[2] *I couldn't get into LINKS because I wasn't qualified. I couldn't do anything in the black community because I wasn't qualified, until every white organization had me on their board. Isn't that something?* It wasn't until prominent citizen Miriam Ortique fought for Leah that she was inducted into LINKS.[3]

A tragedy struck the restaurant in May 1998 and Leah's faith was tested again. At 10:45 P.M., May 1, a man holding a baby, accompanied by the baby's mother, entered the takeout section of the restaurant. Dooky took the man's order for two oyster po' boys and two Cokes and chatted with the couple while the kitchen team prepared the food. Most of the diners inside the restaurant were finishing their meals or had already gone home.

A woman, yelling and wielding a knife, burst through the door of the takeout. Her target was her former lover—the man who had jilted her for another woman, the man holding the baby. The

Leah Chase with model at Ebony *fashion show—fundraiser for Flint-Goodridge Hospital*

woman lunged at the man and swiped him with her knife. Dooky jumped from behind the cash register and grabbed the baby as the man, chased by his attacker, ran outside. Dooky locked the door and dialed 911. The man was murdered.

The publicity following the tragic event was explosive, damning. Some of the victim's family blamed the Chases for pushing the man outside, saying he might be alive if they'd done otherwise. The neighborhood was in an uproar. People said, "Those folks weren't even our people. They came from across the river. What do they expect Mr. Dooky to do? He has to protect his place and his people."

Leah's assessment of the tragic incident was no surprise. *Dooky will be devastated by this for months. Me? I just pray and keep going.* Leah surprises herself sometimes with her reactions to horrible events. *I wonder sometimes if I'm a good Christian. If something terrible happens, and I know I can't do anything about it, it hurts me. People say, 'Oh, you're so strong.' I think strong people hurt just like weaker people— but I don't know. I just have to put it aside and go on.*

Father Mike, priest of St. Peter Claver Catholic Church, has known Leah a long time. "Leah is what I call an old-fashioned church lady. She eats, sleeps, and drinks church. No matter when you talk to her, or no matter what about, somehow, church or God is going to come out. I'll say, 'Leah, I have this event . . .'

'Don't worry, I'll take care of it.'

'Well, how are you going to take care of it?'

'Don't worry. God's going to make a way.' She prays. She's always praying. When she's cooking, she's praying. She's constantly a woman at prayer. Yes, times were tough, but there was a hope grounded in faith. That's how Leah operates. Everything is grounded in her faith. No matter where she goes. She is a committed person. She has endured a lot of suffering and pain. She says God will always find a way. And that's what she really believes."

Few people outside her immediate family know Leah's prayer life as well as her niece and sous-chef, Cleo Robinson. "We've got rosaries all over the place, in the pocket, in the pocketbook, hanging up in places. We got rosaries and we say those rosaries, and when things get rough, she'll say, 'Oh Lord, just get me through the day. Oh Lord, just get me through the day.' And I'll say, 'Oh Lord, it's Leah again.' We pray a lot.

Leah's sister, Janice, wrote a family prayer when a nephew was in a difficult situation, facing a trial by jury. She devised a way to unite the whole family in prayer. She sent copies of the prayer to everyone in the family, asking all to pray at 6:00 P.M. Central Standard Time. Everyone repeated the prayer daily as long as the trial lasted.

> Heavenly Father, we are a family of faith. It is in that faith that we humbly come to you in prayer. You have said, "Ask and you shall receive; knock and it shall be opened unto you. Today we ask for divine guidance to help us choose the path You would have us follow and the courage to fight the battles we now face. We especially pray for _____. We know that as long as we trust in You, nothing is impossible. Our lives are in Your hands. May we live with Your love in our hearts. Amen.

The nephew was acquitted. The attorney said he had never seen a family so strong and united as this family.

*You have to know this man, my nephew. He is a goody two shoes. He'll help anybody—the Indians out in the country. He was going to help people in Africa. We prayed him to freedom. One of my granddaughters didn't eat meat until he was cleared. It lasted a couple of months. We wrote letters to that judge and boy did we celebrate when he was cleared. It worked, honey. She was supposed to be a hard judge. I told her right at the beginning of the whole thing, 'How could you do this to this man? If you do this, I'll never be able to do charity work again. If you could punish **this** man, I just don't know what to think.'*

Family and church are the cores of Leah's strength. Her unwavering Catholic faith and the strong models provided by her parents, particularly her father, teach Leah to develop clear, uncomplicated values, and she operates by those values every day of her life. The act of helping others spins in concentric circles around Leah. What she learned from her parents has been passed on to her children and her grandchildren, and if ever she should falter, all she has to do is pick up the phone and call the nearest sister or brother. *That's one advantage of a big family. There's always somebody there.* One of Leah's sisters lost a daughter when the daughter was twenty-eight. Another sister lost a daughter-in-law when the girl was in her twenties. *We have all felt those pains. So we stick together with all our problems, with everything that goes down. We hang.*

Leah Chase takes risks. She can because of her faith. *You know, fear can destroy you. . . . A lot of people let fear destroy them. I'm never going to be that afraid of anything or anybody. I always say those are faithless people. I have faith in God; I have faith in Leah. Why would any-body want to do me anything?* Leah's words are believable. Her life and its accomplishments are a tribute to her reliance on faith and prayer. It therefore comes as a shock to learn that she has one great fear—death. *I want to get sick and I want to get ready to die. I'm afraid to die. Death frightens me. You know you're going to meet your Maker. How do I know I'm good enough? How do I know that? Nobody has ever come back, and some people tell you, 'Well, you know, God is this and God is that, and God is just,' but well, I don't know if I'm good enough.*

Well-meaning friends have advised Leah to move out of her so-called bad neighborhood. *This isn't a bad neighborhood. The people here would not hurt my customers. They would help them, not hurt them. Now, I'll tell you about the people in this neighborhood. About fif-teen years ago, the Rolling Stones were at the Superdome.*[4] *We were sell-ing concert tickets. You could not sell tickets other than for cash, and tickets were thirty dollars apiece. I told people, 'Look here, I'm not going to baby-sit you so don't come here and stay all night. If you want to be first in line, come around 5:00 A.M.' So they started lining up around 4 or 5—all around the corner, not one black in the whole kit and caboodle out there, all white. And they had to pay cash for their tickets. You know what the neighbors were doing? Going down to the corner and buying papers for the people in line, buying them coffee, buying them dough-nuts. The people were making about fifty cents in tips and stuff, and that's the kind of thing they were doing. Now, these people sat out there. Dark, it was dark when they started lining up. We had no security to watch them; they just sat. We opened at 10, and in one hour, we had sold forty thousand dollars worth of tickets. Do you hear what I'm telling you? In those pockets in this neighborhood out there, there was $40,000. Now the neighbors knew that. They know everything, darling. They know everything that comes on that television. So they knew that these people had to spend cash for these tickets; they knew that. They didn't touch a one—in* **this** *neighborhood.*

To Leah, this is just one more occasion where the Lord steered her through what could have been a problem area. The one area of unfinished business Leah has with the Lord concerns her deceased daughter, Emily. *After Emily died, I prayed, 'Oh, please let her be good*

The Dooky Chase Restaurant is located across the street from the Lafitte Housing Project.

enough; let her be good enough.' As good as I thought she was, I don't know how God looked at her. But people said, 'Leah, God doesn't think like you're thinking. He doesn't.' I said, 'Well how do I know how he's thinking?' We try to live by the rules but we're human and we fall off sometimes.

Family members and friends worry about Leah. Her sisters tell her all the time she works too hard. She shouldn't do this. She shouldn't do that. One sister complains, "You can't talk to Leah. Her feet hurt. Her legs worry her. She takes care of everyone else but she takes care of herself last. She doesn't listen." An old friend remarks, "Can you believe, with all the work she's doing, she will take the time to pray for you? She'll say, 'You can handle it. Are you praying on it? I'll pray with you.' "

Making sacrifices. Taking risks. Helping the community. Leah Chase starts each day talking to God: *Lord, give me the strength to get through the day.* She ends each day saying, *Thank you, Lord—one more day.* They seem to make a good pair, Leah and God. Together, they are changing a neighborhood, a city, and a nation for the betterment of mankind.

CHAPTER EIGHT

Art Smoothes the Edges

A love of beauty and a woman named Celestine Cook led Leah Chase into the art world. Celestine Cook had a much different background. She was younger and from Galveston, Texas, and had graduated from Tuskegee University in Alabama. Her first husband, killed in a plane crash in 1948, was an entrepreneur who had amassed a significant fortune, including real-estate holdings and private airplanes. Celestine and her husband, affluent and cultured, held lavish parties. Should Celestine need assistance with a theme for a party, she would hire consultants from Neiman Marcus.

Well-educated, highly cultivated, gracious, and strong, she quickly established a lifestyle in New Orleans like she had enjoyed in Galveston. She was appointed to numerous boards; she was quick to help people and groups she believed in; she collected art, knew famous artists like Alexander Calder, and worked to promote lesser-known artists, such as Elizabeth Catlett and Gilbert Fletcher; and she was a frequent client at the Dooky Chase Restaurant, where she particularly loved Leah's oysters and fettuccini.

It was only natural that she and Leah Chase aligned themselves. Both strong women who loved to give and to help, they combined their talents for the good of the community. *She was one black person who would do things at her house. The first time I met her was at a fundraiser. She'd use her house to entertain people, to fundraise for different things—Democrats, or whoever was running that she liked, white, black, anything. We worked together for Israel Augustine but later we worked together for Lindy Boggs.[1] The Free Southern Theater had a big thing in her backyard.[2] If ever there was any person who taught me a lot, she did. She taught me how to do fancy things. When Liberty Bank opened, she was on their board and they had a party.[3] She said, 'Now, Leah's going to do this party.' I didn't know how to do those things, but she guided me. She told me what to serve and how to do special things.*

When Rose Loving ran for the school board, Celestine said, 'Leah, we have to do this.[4] We have to get Rose elected to the school board.' So we worked for Rose Loving and she was the first black woman on the New Orleans Public School Board. Then, Celestine was on the board at the New Orleans Museum of Art. She's the person who brought me in to see Jacob Lawrence. And she's the one responsible for getting me appointed to the museum board, too.

Leah became active at the museum at about the same time another young black woman in New Orleans, Bobbie Dent, opened an art gallery on Dumaine Street, the Nexus Gallery. Mrs. Dent had been with the Schomburg Collection in New York City and brought her expertise back home.[5] Local black artists were enthusiastic about having a gallery where their work would be shown. Artists like Clifton Webb and John Scott approached Mayor Dutch Morial and encouraged him to put art on the civic agenda.[6] At the same time, they lobbied Leah Chase to help their cause.

Clifton Webb was only twenty-five years old when he became one of the founders of the Contemporary Arts Center. He sensed a lack of dialogue and organization among black artists in the community and wanted to do something to change that. Once again, the Dooky Chase Restaurant became a meeting place for action, but this time, the objective was to promote the art of local black artists. Scott and Martin Payton joined Webb: "A national meeting of African-American artists was to be held in New Orleans. We wanted to have a gathering, so we invited everybody to dinner at the Dooky Chase Restaurant. We were in the upstairs room and Leah did all the food. It was a fantastic time. It was like the starting point of something. Mel Edwards, a nationally known sculptor, gave Mrs. Chase a drawing. After that, artists were coming in on a regular basis." *I met Mel Edwards when we had an art conference here. All those artists . . . they signed the back of my book. I had David Driskell, Mel Edwards, Raymond Saunders, all the biggies, in there for a gumbo party.[7]*

Clifton Webb

Leah Chase and Clifton Webb go way back. As a university student at Louisiana State University in the late sixties, Webb would visit his grandmother in New Orleans and they would eat at the restaurant. "We were regulars at the place, and we got to know her and love her." When Webb married and moved to New Orleans, he and his wife dined at the restaurant and talked at length with Miss Chase "about art, life, and social situations." It was the beginning of a long relationship. The first drawing Webb gave Leah still hangs in the Gold Room. Today, several of his pieces hang on her walls and one of his sculptures stands in a prominent place in the Victorian Room. *Clifton is good to me. He frames things for me, hangs them. His wife, Jo, has a degree in art history and she does some of the mattings. He's brought me a lot. They've both helped me, advised me.*

Leah's importance in the world of art is not restricted to New Orleans. In 1995 the National Endowment for the Arts was under fire from many conservative legislators, and its budget was likely to suffer a big cut. Leah was called upon to testify before a subcommittee of the Appropriations Committee of the United States House of Representatives. When she stood to address the group, she was speaking on behalf of the New Orleans Museum of Art, the Association of Art Museum Directors, the American Arts Alliance, and the American Association of Museums. She tossed away the speech her son had helped her write and spoke to the committee from her heart:

> In 1978 . . . I was fifty-five years old and had never set foot in a museum before. . . . I was born a country girl. Sure, I saw strawberries but not in a painting; I had to pick them to help my family earn a living for me and my ten sisters and brothers. . . . Art serves all communities. My life experience provides evidence that refutes the allegation that federal money for the arts benefits only higher-income people. I am by no means as poor as I once was when picking strawberries, but I am by no means among the rich and famous, either. For me, support for the arts is an investment in the artistic excellence of my people . . . who, like me, needed to see something beautiful and breathtaking in order to aspire to higher things. . . . Art softens people up and warms them up to deal with each other in humane ways. . . . We need your continued help.[8]

The collection she has assembled on the walls of her restaurant is unique. John Bullard, director of the New Orleans Museum of Art (NOMA), regularly brings out-of-town guests to lunch at Leah's to meet her and to see her personal collection. Stella Jones, owner of the Stella Jones Gallery in New Orleans, says, "Before I opened my gallery in 1994, the Dooky Chase Restaurant was THE gallery for black artists in New Orleans."

When she talks about her art collection, Leah gets excited. *I could be as mean as a sack of rattlesnakes if I didn't have this art to soften me up.* Her sous-chef, Cleo, says her love of art even affects her work in the kitchen. "When she's working on something for the museum, or for a group of artists, she's softer, more easygoing. I think it relaxes her."

Leah Chase's work in the art world has not always been relaxed. When the World Exposition of 1984 was preparing its opening in New Orleans, Leah was a member of a committee planning its art exhibition. The purpose of the exhibition was to exhibit Louisiana's artists, particularly New Orleans' artists. An art expert served as juror and selected the pieces to be shown. When the dust settled,

Left to right: *John Scott, Leah Chase, Janel Nelson, David Driskell*

Leah Chase testifying before the subcommittee of the U.S. House of Representatives, courtesy Rick Reinhard, Washington, D.C.

John Bullard and Leah Chase

only one black artist was represented in the group, and he was a self-taught artist from Patterson, Louisiana, David Butler. As word got out, members of the black community became enraged, not the least of whom was Mayor Dutch Morial. Local artist John Scott threatened to sue the committee and the exhibition. The dilemma set heavily on Leah's heart. After all, the juror was an expert and had been given a job to do. He did it. The committee couldn't just throw his work out and start over. And yet, just as heavily for Leah was the realization that a number of talented, educated, renowned artists, at this once-in-a-lifetime event, would not have the opportunity to be represented. She had to act.

You got the whole eyes of the country, of the world, on you, and you're sixty percent black, and you're going to ignore the talented artists we have here? Depict your black people like a bunch of ignoramuses? You can't do that. A member of the committee remembers Leah's action and states unequivocally, "She could act because she's a *grande dame* and because she's gracious and sincere." *I went to every meeting. I didn't want to deny anybody anything, didn't want to put down the gentleman hired to jury the show. So how do you handle this?* The solution chosen was to run a parallel exhibition of art, juried by a committee. The art of several local artists was selected and in Leah's opinion: *It really turned out to be a good show.* Not everyone agreed with the solution, however. Twenty years later some members of the original committee shrug their shoulders, raise their eyebrows and plead ignorance or a bad memory when asked to comment on the exhibition.

With the help of friends in the art world, Leah Chase has filled the walls of her restaurant with art. She worried about the aesthetic positioning of some of the paintings until local art critic Luba Glade gave her some advice: "Put it all over. You don't have to put it this way or that way, just put it all over." That's what she has done.

Courtesy of Gavin Goins, Goins Photography

This is a woodcut done by Sue Jane Smock. Woodcuts amaze me. You have to carve it out and put the ink on it and then press. Sue Jane was working at the museum and the volunteers bought this as a gift for me. But I like this, a mother with children. That's the way children are, always . . . one in the arms and one hanging on.

Courtesy of Gavin Goins, Goins Photography

*This is a Ron Adams piece. I call it **The Fisherman**. I got this through the Stella Jones Gallery. Ron had a show there. This is the way they sell me art. Ron said, 'Go put this on her wall.' Then they send me the bill. . . . Look at that face. That face is grotesque in a way. And when I look at that body and think about men who lift weights these days to get those kind of muscles. . . . That man never lifted a weight in his life. He just lifted up his boat when he got ready to move; lifted everything around him to survive and get his work done. That face says, 'I'm just a simple man, doing what I do.' And I like that.*

Courtesy of Gavin Goins, Goins Photography

This is a Richard Thomas. This is everybody's favorite piece; it's a fun piece. The title is **Like This**. This little boy is teaching him to play that horn and he's got all the wrong posture. Nobody is supposed to huff like that when they're blowing. It's fun . . . two little kids. Everybody thinks that's Wynton [Marsalis]. It isn't.

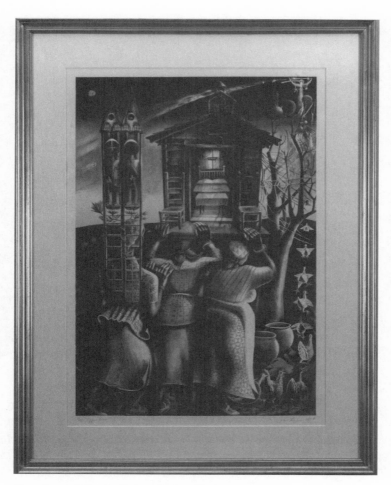

Courtesy of Gavin Goins, Goins Photography

[This is] John Biggers' Upper Room. John is kinda a religious man and there is an upper room series in the Bible. And John adds what he wants. I like what John does with women. His admiration for women is unbelievable. He appreciates women, admires them, their strength and all, and it's depicted here a lot. He'd have to explain what he means with those chickens all over the place; but because he goes way back to his mother and his grandmother, and they were always washing clothes, you will always find a wash pot and a washboard in John's work. Here's the washboard. Look at her dress, corrugated like the washboard. It's beautiful.

Courtesy of Gavin Goins, Goins Photography

That's a Jake Lawrence. He did that in 1975, Confrontation on the Bridge at Selma, Alabama. *The dog depicts the policeman, driving the people back. You know, John Lewis is from Atlanta, and he's in the House of Representatives in Washington. And he comes and he says, 'Leah, I was on that bridge.' You have fun when you have somebody who can relate to the painting.*

Courtesy of Gavin Goins, Goins Photography

See those little faces? They're angels. See the beautiful little faces. I got that from Stella Jones. Now, Stella just comes in and hangs it up. So you see what's happening? See that empty space beside it? Now I have to go buy another piece because the wall is unbalanced.

Courtesy of Gavin Goins, Goins Photography

*This is Bill Hudson. I got this piece years ago when Celestine was still living. She called me to her house. She said, 'Leah, you got to see this. You just drop everything and come now.' So I went to her house and saw this work on the floor. I didn't know anything, but **she** knew. It was called [the] Sea, Sky and Land series, from off the coast of Africa where he was living. I thought the colors were beautiful. I got this piece when he was artist in residence at LSU (Louisiana State University).*

Courtesy of Gavin Goins, Goins Photography

Gilbert Fletcher did a series of old houses, and this is called—just like the houses were called in those days—The Cribs. They were one-room houses and they were really in the red-light district. You almost feel somebody getting ready to look out that window, with the curtains playing in that window. Isn't that wonderful? Elle magazine came through here one time and they did a whole article on this restaurant—this restaurant and three or four others. Then the magazine came out. I saw what they had done with the other restaurants and I was not included. 'Oh well,' I said. 'She worked here for three days, but maybe she just couldn't do it. Whatever.' Nothing in the magazine on Dooky Chase . . . the next month, I got five pages in Elle magazine. Wasn't that wonderful? They lowered this painting down to a table and put a plate of chicken in front of it and photographed it. I was so proud of that.

Courtesy of Gavin Goins, Goins Photography

This painting tells a story. There's a tale written in it. Claire Foster Burnett is the artist. She came up to me at my birthday party at the museum and said, 'I want you to have this.[9] And I want to tell you why I want you to have this.' She said, 'I remember when I was a little girl my mother used to go to the restaurant just to talk to you. I used to sit way in the corner while you talked in the other corner with my mother. I never forgot that.' I remember her mother, Mrs. Foster, a little dark lady, pleasant woman, always smiling, and she used to be a social worker. She was having a few problems and she'd come and talk to me. Now, there was nothing I could tell her, you know. But I just listened and talked with her. So here it is, written on this painting: 'Once many years ago you took time out of your busy schedule to have a tete-a-tete with a friend of mine. This collage was created for you in thankfulness for that linkage. Wishing you the best always, Sincerely, Claire Foster Burnett. . . . Erma's daughter.' You wouldn't think a child would remember, you know?

Leah and longtime friend, Sunny Normand, at Leah's seventy-fifth birthday party/fundraiser at the New Orleans Museum of Art

Courtesy of Gavin Goins, Goins Photography

That would have to be everybody's favorite: Elizabeth Catlett. If you go back in my day when those people went to church on Sunday . . . I know that's where she was going because she has a hat on, and that was called a Panama, a white Panama straw. It had either a blue or a black band on it. Every old lady had one of those. You didn't change your hat every year. You might buy a hat every five years. You wore it to church on Sunday and then you went home and put it back in the box and it went back in the armoire. You had a summer hat and a winter hat. And when you had that hat on, that meant you were really going places, to church or whatever. And that little boy walking there, she's saying to him, 'Boy, we're going to church. You behave. You don't say a word.' . . . Today they have bathrooms in the back of the church. In my day, my daddy took us to the church. You GO before you leave home. Don't say a word. Once you get to church, you have to sit in church. Don't say a word in church. And we didn't. Other children might be cutting up. No. Daddy said if you talked or made any noise in church, you were going to get it when you got home. And you better not look like you need to go to the bathroom. Oh my God. No indeed! You sat there, and you wore the best things you had. You had to dress up to go to church because he always told you, 'You not going to go to any place bigger than to church, because this is the house of God. There's no place bigger than that.' Whatever was your best clothes, that's what you put on to go to church on Sunday. So that [painting] reminds me of church.

Courtesy of Gavin Goins, Goins Photography

That big piece in the center is Ron Bechet. Ron belongs to the big musical family, Sidney Bechet's people. Those are his people. He's head of the Art Department at Xavier University. I went to the Stern Gallery and I told the lady there, 'I really like this, but I don't have the money for it.' Next thing, [it was] on the wall. Then comes a statement from the company they work with. I just pay once a month. I learned that's a nice way to get what you want.

Courtesy of Gavin Goins, Goins Photography

This is a white artist . . . named Strickland. Everybody likes that and I love it. Celestine gave that to me, too. It was in her house and she always liked it. She sent it to me before she died. She said, 'I want you to have this because I know you like it.' I said, 'I like it because the woman comes through so strong.' And you have to understand the strength of black women in those days. For some uncanny reason, people respected them. They would call them Aunt So-and-So, Aunt Jane, whatever. All the whites would call her Aunt Jane, but honey, Aunt Jane could do anything she wanted. . . . Those poor little men. They [are] standing there so meek and humble. But look at the sister, honey. 'I dare you to mess this. You weigh this right.'

Courtesy of Gavin Goins, Goins Photography

That's my favorite Elizabeth Catlett—so strong. She's just telling the sisters, 'Come on. We're moving. We're gone.'

Courtesy of Gavin Goins, Goins Photography

That little piece is the first piece I ever owned by Clifton Webb—that little drawing. And I liked it. I keep it up because it's the first thing I ever had that Clifton brought to me. Clifton has helped me a lot.

Courtesy of Gavin Goins, Goins Photography

That piece is Caruso's Grocery. That's by Gilbert Fletcher, too. We had Italian groceries on almost every corner in the black community. I did a book signing in Bay St. Louis, Mississippi, and these people bought my book. The lady came back to me and said, 'That's my grandfather's grocery!' She was so happy. Every time that family comes to New Orleans they come here to dinner, and they see their grandfather's grocery. The husband says, 'Miss Chase, those were good days. We used to sell those backbones.' And we learned to cook those backbones and made the nicest gravies with them. So you see, it was a learning thing between the two cultures, the Italian and the African-American cultures.

Leah's art collection is like a storybook. Painting after painting, like page after page in a book, tells a story. The story is about Leah Chase and how she has championed the arts, for her people and for all people, a story about her love for art and artists' love for her, a story of how, once again, one person can make a difference.

CHAPTER NINE

Forty Ducks and Dutch

If Celestine Cook was Leah Chase's mentor in the world of art, Dutch Morial was her soul mate in the world of community action. Both bright, involved, on the move, and ambitious, they were drawn to each other as surely as moths to a candlewick. Their differences were just as pronounced as their similarities. Morial was boisterous, powerful, highly educated, and at the forefront of most things political in the city. Leah was quieter, softer, kinder, working behind the scenes.

As a younger man, Dutch Morial was an attorney active with the Frontiers, a men's social club. The group met monthly and planned activities for the community, and when they met, they ate, in the upstairs dining room at Dooky Chase. *They'd talk about events coming up and honoring people, and Dutch was a thorn in their side. He'd tell them, 'You can't do this' and 'I'm going to do this,' and 'No, that's not what you do.' They couldn't understand Dutch. Dutch wanted to go faster, do more.*

One point Leah Chase and Dutch Morial agreed on in those early days was the issue of voting practices. They opposed the common but demeaning action of black voters voting for white politicians who paid for their votes. Just as avidly, they opposed block voting. They didn't accept the practice of voting for someone just because that person was black, when so many people had fought so hard to give blacks the right to vote, period. *You gonna sell me down the drain for this? Let me do for myself. Don't tell me how to vote.* As an attorney, Morial was constantly defending Civil Rights activists. He was firmly committed to the goals of the NAACP and became president of the New Orleans chapter in

Attorney Ernest "Dutch" Morial (left), at a Frontier Club meeting in the Upstairs Room

1962. He was an honest and nonmilitant Civil Rights leader, becoming Louisiana's first black U. S. attorney in 1965. By 1978, he was mayor of New Orleans.

While Morial's friendship with Leah Chase started at her table as a result of those early Frontier Club meetings, it grew into a strong alliance. They made a good pair. When Sybil Morial got tired of her husband's ducks taking up room in her freezer, Dutch took them to Leah. "We're going to cook up these ducks, have a big supper, and invite all my friends." *That's when we had the upstairs. Now, that upstairs was something else again. So he had the dinner up there. He brought forty ducks and we had about forty men. A lot of his cronies, political people, were there. I went to see Charlie Hutchinson and said, 'Come on, we have to make this fun.'[1] So I borrowed some of his decoys and I set up a swamp scene up there. It was really pretty. We did the ducks and I furnished whatever—the greens, rice dressing, cornbread dressing, sweet potatoes, and turnips. You have to have turnips with those wild ducks. But that meeting was red hot.*

It was red hot because it was 1979, the eve of a threatened police union strike that would coincide with the biggest party New Orleans ever throws—Mardi Gras. Dutch Morial was chief executive officer of a police force that was only twenty percent black and two percent female. He had hired an out-of-town police supervisor, going against the grain of the traditional practice of hiring from within. The city council, while voting itself a raise, had cut sick leave, annual leave, and other fringe benefits enjoyed by members of the police force. Tension was at an all-time high, and the trump card played by the police union was a walkout during Mardi Gras.

Morial was faced with enormous problems. Cancellation of Mardi Gras would cost the city, by some estimates, two hundred and fifty million dollars. Going ahead with Mardi Gras would mean employing state police and National Guardsmen at a projected cost of one hundred thousand dollars per day.[2] The city was in an uproar. Mardi Gras krewe leaders were nervous. On everyone's minds was one thing—the question of safety versus economic loss.

That night, tempers flared over Leah's duck dinner. Messages between the police teamsters union and the mayor's dinner party came and went: *'You can go tell so-and-so . . .' 'I'm not going to be your runner; you go tell him yourself.' . . . and back and forth. So I said, 'Look, this is too hot for me. I'm leaving.' There were never any women at these duck dinners. Never! This was a stag thing. But that was a fun one that night.*

On February 17, nearly twelve hundred police officers walked off the job. The mayor canceled all parades scheduled for that Saturday, plus Sunday and Monday. On Sunday, February 18, Carnival krewe captains canceled all parades for the 1979 Mardi Gras season. *Dutch had a good rapport with the Uptown people and he worked on that. It was touch and go for a long time. Then I remember, everybody, they said, 'We'll cancel Mardi Gras.' The Rex people. Comus.*[3] *Now, that was a big thing. It was a feather in Dutch's cap that he was able to get those people to cancel Carnival. And it was very gracious of them, too. But those were the big men. So they canceled Carnival.* By the time Mardi Gras ended, the public was almost universally behind the mayor, blaming the police and the teamsters for destroying their Mardi Gras.

Leah Chase's duck dinners for Dutch Morial became an annual

event, and despite their future addition of other game, from tuna to squirrels, they were always called duck dinners. Growing in size and needing bigger space, the dinners moved from Leah's restaurant to Gallier Hall, but Leah still cooked. In 1985, the duck dinners had to be moved from Gallier Hall, which was closed for renovation, to the Municipal Auditorium.[4] It was relatively small, accommodating about only two hundred people. The most important memory Leah has of that dinner was Dutch's being in a vile mood. *Dutch's mood . . . the worst mood I've ever seen Dutch in was at that dinner. When Dutch wanted something, he could be pretty ugly sometime, and that rubbed some people the wrong way.* One guest at this dinner had spent a large sum of money supporting a candidate who was running for the city council against the person Morial was quietly supporting. *Honey, he chewed [that man] up, down, and over. Man left the duck dinner because Dutch had really eaten him alive. He was rip-roaring ugly. He was ready to chew **me** up and I said, 'Hey, this is me.'*

The biggest duck dinner, by far, brought together over six hundred people and was held at the Greek Hellenic Center. It was in 1986, Dutch's last year in office. Dutch's friends showed up at the duck dinner with big banners boldly stating Run Dutch Run, Run Dutch Run. But Dutch couldn't run. A city ordinance prevented his running for mayor again and he was supporting his protégé, Donald Mintz.

Leah and her daughter, Emily, backed up by Leah's niece, Cleo, worked for three days preparing for this dinner. *We didn't do anything half-stepping for Dutch. He didn't like anything half-stepping. You're not going to serve Dutch anything in a paper cup. You'll put six hundred glasses down on that table. You'll put six hundred wineglasses on that table and you're going to put good china on that table. You're going to do it **right** for Dutch Morial.* Emily would take a crew in the morning and set up everything, then Leah would come with the food. *So I got there and there was this white girl on the floor working the bar. She was a sweetheart, but I had to tell her she couldn't work that bar—no women on the floor. So she came back in the kitchen and helped us there. She carved the turkey.*

Then here comes somebody and says, 'Miss Kelso is here.'[5]

Emily Chase Haydel and Leah Chase

'Well,' I said, 'She's got to go. No women come to this party. She's got to go.' So I went out there and I said, 'I'm sorry, you have to leave.'

She said, 'Leah, you're going to put me out?'

'Yep,' I said, 'we said, no women here.'

She said, 'But Dutch invited me.'

I said, 'Dutch, come here. You invited her?'

'Yes Leah. . . . You know why? She said she was going to write about all of us and our duck dinner.'

I said, 'Aw shucks, all right, go sit down.' So we let Iris stay. All those six hundred men and Iris out on the floor. I tore poor Iris loose that night and I thought she would come back at me. You'd think she'd say something. She never said a thing. I called her later and said, 'I'm sorry. I was just teasing you.'

They loved the food. We had food unbelievable. We had rows of chafing dishes. We had fried turkey. We had cochon de lait [suckling pig], fried alligator, alligator sauce piquant, quail, rabbit, venison. I cooked about one hundred and fifty pheasants, wild duck, tame duck. We had about everything you can mention at this party.

Niece Cleo remembers the dinner vividly: "We had people from every walk of life bringing stuff. One man pulled up in his truck with ducks and pheasants, squirrels, rabbits. One man came in his truck with tuna and shrimp, salmon. We had pigs. Anything that was walking in the woods, we had it. We had to clean it all and prepare it. We had so much, we said, 'Well, we've stewed this one, we fried that one, we've fricasseed this one, now what are we going to do with that one?' It got to the point we just started putting it together and giving it a name. Finally everything that was little, we threw it in a gumbo and called it Critter Gumbo. We invented a lot. And then we had all the side dishes: smothered turnips, mustard greens, sweet potatoes, cornbread, jambalaya, macaroni. That's what they wanted."

*The day of the party, Emily called me and said, 'Mother, you're not going to believe this. There's a truck at the back door.' What's in the truck? Two wild boars from snoot to tail, whole; two whole alligators just with the heads cut off; two huge tunas like you wouldn't believe—whole. I never did a tuna before, never cleaned a tuna before—that was fun, getting to that; fifty pounds of the most beautiful shrimp you ever saw; venison steaks; a truckful! I said, 'Look, we can't do anything with that now. Put it in the freezer. **Put it in the freezer.** We're going to this party.'*

WILD DUCKS AND TURNIPS

2 wild ducks	3 cups water
2 tbsp. garlic, chopped	1 cup onion, chopped
Salt and black pepper	2 sprigs fresh thyme
1/4 cup flour	2 large turnips, diced
1/2 tsp. paprika	1/2 tsp. white pepper
1/4 tsp. garlic powder	1 tbsp. parsley, chopped
6 strips bacon	

Ducks should be picked well; no feathers should be left on the birds. Pass birds over an open flame on stove; this will singe small feathers. Hold birds under running water, rubbing them briskly to remove all small feathers. Wipe ducks dry. Raise the skin on breast of ducks; rub 1 tablespoon of the chopped garlic under duck skin. Mix salt and pepper. Season ducks by rubbing mixture in cavity of ducks and over the entire birds.

Mix flour, paprika, and garlic powder. Dredge the ducks in the flour mixture. Set birds aside.

Cut bacon in small pieces. In a small Magnalite roaster or Dutch oven, cook bacon pieces until the fat is rendered. Remove cooked bacon from pot. Place prepared ducks in pot, breast side up. Brown ducks on all sides. Add water, onions, remaining garlic, and thyme. Cover tightly and let simmer for 1 hour, turning as ducks cook. When ducks are tender, pour turnips around ducks. Add white pepper, parsley, and bacon pieces. Cover pot and let simmer until turnips are done—about 20 minutes. Yield: 4 servings.

One week before he died, Dutch went to Leah's for lunch, sat at his normal table, number five, and reflected out loud about his children. He told Leah, "Look at my children. I got one that's a lawyer, one that's in insurance, one that's a banker, but Leah, what am I going to do with that little one?" She was a good athlete, a "jock," according to Dutch, but it was her he worried about most.

Leah listened. *You don't need to worry about that one. She's just like you. She'll be the one to take care of you. You don't worry about her. She's going to be okay.* Dutch was excited because all his children would be home for Christmas. He was planning to cook a big dinner.

Then I said, 'What you gonna do, Dutch?'

And he said, 'Don't you worry about me, you go support Donald [Mintz].'

I said, 'Well, I have to know what you're going to do.'

He said, 'I'm not going to do anything. You help Donald. My wife and I, we're going to New York. We're going to the NAACP banquet.'

We were just good friends, just good friends. He would always include me in whatever he was doing. I would do anything for him and he knew it. But I didn't expect one thing from Dutch Morial. I didn't expect that and I didn't ask him for anything. Like today, people vote for you because they expect you to do something for them. No, I'm doing what I can do for you so you can do your job. Your job is to help all of us. That's all I did for Dutch, but I knew him, and I liked him.

Ernest "Dutch" Morial died on December 24, 1989, at the age of sixty. Leah is certain he had bigger things in mind. *He was going for the biggie. He knew he could never win here again, but he said, 'Look at Governor Wilder in Virginia.[6] We can do the same thing in this state.' He didn't say, 'I could run.' I said, 'Well you take a rest and we'll see; we'll see.' He wasn't the kind of man who was going to quit. He couldn't do that. It was just in him, that drive. That's what I really loved about him, that drive. He would just go and go and never give up. He would never have gone to run the NAACP. There wasn't enough battle in that.*

Others came here and they asked me to continue the duck dinners but I said, 'No, I can't do that.' I couldn't do that. I did all that for Dutch. All that food and everything. . . . I did a lot of things with Dutch—a lot of things. But that was my way of helping. Dutch was the one with the brains. Dutch could get things done, and that's what you have to do. You don't want a leader who can't get ideas and stand on his own with everybody. Dutch could stand on his own with everybody. He could reach back and pull up that second effort. That's what I loved about Dutch.

CHAPTER TEN

A Bunch of Cayoudles

When a marketing representative for Kraft Foods called Leah to ask if the Chase family would be interested in filming a commercial of a big family barbecue, Leah's youngest daughter, also named Leah, joked, "Ha! When they see us, they won't want us. We're a bunch of cayoudles."

Cayoudle is an expression used to describe a dog that exhibits many different physical traits; his pedigree is impossible to pin down. To simply call it a mixed breed is to understate the complex lineage the dog represents. In the sense of complex lineage, Leah's family proudly crosses all the colors of the familiar child's song: "Red and yellow, black and white . . ." and several shades in between. Black American, white American, Asian-American, American Indian, and Creole are all represented in the family. This wasn't always the case. Leah's own heritage is *Creole de couleur,* a term used to describe a specific group of people who live in New Orleans and in other Southern cities. When Leah was a young woman, Creoles married only other Creoles.

Historically, the word *creole* has been interchangeable as a noun or an adjective and has created a great deal of confusion. According to some scholars, its origin lies in the Portuguese word *crioulo,* a term used to designate a slave of African descent born in the New World.[1] But as scholar Gwendolyn Midlo Hall writes, that meaning was expanded: "In Spanish and French colonies, including eighteenth-century Louisiana, the term *Creole* was used to distinguish American-born from African-born slaves; first generation slaves born in America and their descendants were designated Creoles."

Late in the eighteenth century, native-born Louisianians began calling themselves *Creoles* for another reason. They wanted to differentiate themselves from foreign born and Anglo-American residents. This group of so-called Creoles included white, black, and mixed-race individuals. By the latter part of the eighteenth century, the number of mixed-race children born of European-African parentage had grown to the point that they formed a distinct cultural group and began referring to themselves as *Creoles of color*.[2] Leah Chase's ancestors were among this group.

The thousands of free people of color living in New Orleans in the 1800s had an important role in the development of the *Creole-de-couleur* community. Identified as neither black nor white, slave nor really free, they worshiped in the St. Louis Cathedral, attended the opera and theater, and spoke French. With light skin, long straight hair, and French surnames, they often held more status than some whites and were therefore despised. On the other hand, they were considered arrogant by the darker-skinned members of their own race.

Describing how that cultural group manifests itself in the city of New Orleans in modern times, writer and researcher Mary Gehman defines Creole as follows:

> Creole can best be defined today as a state of mind and of heritage. It means being Catholic, a parishioner of Corpus Christi, St. Augustine or St. Leo the Great churches and sending one's children to parochial schools like St. Mary's, Xavier Prep or St. Aug. It means membership in one of the social clubs like the Autocrat or the Original Illinois. Family comes first with close attention paid to observing birthdays, baptisms and First Communions; holidays are invariably spent together. Most Creole children have a *Marraine* and/or *Parraine*, godmother and godfather, who take their roles seriously. It means having heard basic French or Creole phrases as a child and peppering one's speech with terms like *compere* or *commere*, meaning close friend, *galerie* for porch or balcony, *banquette* for sidewalk and *tisane* for a medicinal tea. It means cooking a great gumbo, making groceries (going to the supermarket) or going to the quarters (visiting the French Quarter), and referring to two o'clock in the afternoon as evening.

Leah Chase grew up and lived among this Creole world. *Beansy Fauria's house was in this neighborhood. He was a black man, but you wouldn't know that if you saw him. He was very elegant, walked with a cane. His family-owned Fauria Awning Business. He owned the Astoria and the Pelican Club on South Rampart Street, plus a couple of lottery companies. A lot of gambling went on over there. Everybody knew Beansy was black. But you'd go to the Orpheum Theater . . . there was the colored entrance, but Beansy would go in by the front door. Nobody said a word.*

Leah has vivid memories of particular Creole customs. When Creoles went to church, they loved to pray and rub, touch, or even kiss the statue of the Blessed Mother. Statues became dirty and worn from so many hands touching them. Although Leah's mother never did this, her paternal grandmother did. This grandmother never got dressed without pinning her Sacred Heart badge to her underwear. It had been given to her by her church, and she wore it religiously.

And Creole ladies used to sell callas. Those sweet rice cakes; they looked like drop doughnuts dusted with powdered sugar. The ladies would walk around with baskets full of the cakes and cry out, 'Callas, bells, and chauds.' People don't make them anymore. They've just lost the knack.

Creoles of color were by definition Afro-European. For the most part, they married one another, often times entering marriages that had been arranged between families. The brown paper-bag test did exist, if not physically, at least mentally. When a light-skinned young man or woman brought a date home to meet the parents, the date had better be no darker than a common, brown, paper grocery bag. Light skin and dark skin did not mix. *If you lived here, you were from Treme.[3] You were Creole here, but don't go beyond Treme, cross that track, beyond Bienville Street. Those were "those Americans," dark-skinned people. You didn't go there and hang around. People ask me, 'Where are the Creoles?' I tell them, 'Well, those Creole girls crossed those tracks and married those Americans . . . end of Creoles, honey.'*

Creole stories in New Orleans make for high drama in their retelling. A Creole man passing for white married his wife only to learn they had both been "passing." Neither knew the other was black. When competitive sports began to be integrated in the Catholic schools, that is to say, black teams playing against white teams, two cousins of Creole origin found themselves playing against each other, one for the white team and one for the black team. A beautiful Creole girl committed the most unpardonable act, not marrying a white man but marrying a non-Catholic. She moved up North and never had children.

Leah's opinions about skin color are as clearly pronounced as her opinions about anything else. *My mother taught us you couldn't make differences in people because they were different colors. She didn't like that at all. Now, I'm going to tell you. I went to St. Mary's Academy, and I don't care how many sisters there were, they were biased. When I was there, there was one family that was really black. All the rest were Creole or very fair. Those dark girls were really discriminated against. I have yet to see a black Miss St. Mary's Academy.*

At one time, the black community of New Orleans was traditionally categorized as Uptown or Downtown, each having distinct differences, the major one being color.[4] Historically, Uptown was dark and Protestant. Downtown was light and Catholic. Downtowners considered the Uptown folks as backward, less educated, and lower class. When Leah was a young woman, there were sections of Uptown where Downtown women didn't go. *You didn't go on Rampart Street. The men went there to gamble. It was weird when you think about it. Yes, they had darker skin, but you had some Uptown people who were class acts. I remember battling the so-called Creoles within my mind. I hated it. I always hated people with an air about themselves, who thought they were better than anyone else. What makes you think that? We're all just people out here.*

In the 1940s, the Treme area housed a mixed-race population. Leah noted the difference in the Creoles living there. *This was a mixed neighborhood, a lot of Creoles, what I call Treme Creoles. The Creoles in the Seventh Ward were different or considered themselves different [from] the Treme Creoles. A lot of the Seventh Ward Creoles spoke fluent French. My mother-in-law didn't speak fluent French; she spoke that real Creole stuff, like a patois.*

Lawrence Otis Graham, in his book, *Our Kind of People*, devotes a section to New Orleans Creoles and notes some of the intricacies involved in tracing their origins. In describing one "slender, small-boned, light-complexioned black woman," he notes, "It seems to be well-established that the wealthy Creoles . . . who come from her background live in downtown New Orleans, while the working-class blacks . . . reside uptown and the working-class Creoles stay in 'back-o'-town.'"

Another person told Graham, "You've never seen class warfare until you've come to New Orleans. . . . There are the Creoles—who might be very, very poor and uneducated, or there's the group of Creoles who are rich and who may be either white-looking or black-looking. . . . Historically, there was so much mixing in that town, you find people with relatives of every shade."

Leah Chase set about in her usual way to pick and choose the traits she would adapt from her own Creole heritage. *They had so many good things about them. They were beautiful to look at, they were good seamstresses, they could do a lot of things, and they had a lot of things going for them. And they were good cooks. Every Creole woman took pride in her gumbo making.*

While the word *Creole* became a loosely applied adjective describing everything from ponies to tomatoes, it was Creole cuisine that launched Leah Chase into the limelight. She refuses to call herself a chef because she has had no formal training. Her professional peers disagree. Famous chef John D. Folse of Lafitte's Landing Restaurant has this to say about Leah Chase:

"What are the definitions of a chef and a cook? Leah is a chef's chef and a cook's cook. She's cooked for more people in power, celebrities; she's cooked for more conventions and conferences; she's talked to more television reporters; she's been on many radio shows; she's written books on the subject. . . . My God. What is a chef? A chef is a leader in the kitchen. A chef is a manager of food and culinary technique and philosophy. A cook is a technician, the person with the skills to make something happen in a pot. And a chef and a cook come together to wow the palette of the guests in the dining room. Is Leah a chef or a cook? She's both, and a whole lot more."

No two people seem to agree on the definition of Creole cuisine. Rudy Lombard in *Creole Feast* stated, "It is difficult to arrive at a universally satisfying definition of Creole cuisine. All such attempts in the past have failed to achieve a consensus, and have seldom been used twice; . . . The single, lasting characteristic of Creole cuisine is the Black element."[5] Lombard was talking about the "black hand in the pot." On this point, Leah agrees. *Creole cooking definitely has an African base.* At the same time, she is amazed at the various renditions of so-called Creole cuisine in the city of New Orleans. *A lot of people got it wrong. Creoles don't use as much tomatoes as people think. I never saw a meatball in red gravy until I came to New Orleans and discovered Italian meatballs. Our meatballs were always in brown gravy. On the other hand, our cuisine came from the islands when the slaves came here. My gumbo is typical Creole gumbo—crab, shrimp, chicken, two kinds of sausage, veal brisket, ham, and a roux, but not a dark roux. The roux has to be just the right color and the right texture. You have to use the very best products you can buy. You have to have Vaucresson chaurice, the best smoked sausage, lean ham, and lean veal.*

Creoles always use onion and garlic and paprika, and lots of green peppers. Even if they make a brown gravy, they put in a little paprika. That makes the gravy glow. If you're cooking beans, you don't just throw those beans on to boil. Just cover the beans, then keep adding water. When the beans get soft, put a skillet with a little oil or fat and fry the sausage or ham. Creoles do not like to see whole beans floating around in that pot. Beans have to be creamy. Cut that seasoning real fine. You're not supposed to see that seasoning, no onions floating in the gravy. And the gravy has to be the right texture. If it's too sticky and gooey, it's called cataplase *[from the French word,* cataplasme, *which means thick and indigestible]. Don't give me that; brown that roux. Don't give me that sticky gravy. Creole cooks take their time. They are very ticky about their food. No matter what they cook, they never cook in a hurry. And they cook things to death. Okra—cook it down, nothing crunchy in Creole cooking. And they never boil cabbage; they smother it. Fry the meat and onions, then put the chunks of cabbage in.*

One of the biggest Creole events at the Dooky Chase Restaurant is the annual Gumbo des Herbes feast, served traditionally on Holy Thursday. A unique and chunky soup, this dish is intended to tide devout Catholics over to Easter Sunday, when they can officially break their Easter fast. According to custom, an odd number of greens must be used and they must be ground or chopped, then boiled. Leah uses eleven types of greens: mustard, collard, turnip, kale, Swiss chard, cabbage, carrot tops, beet tops, watercress, spinach, and pepper grass. *Used to be an old lady who walked in the neutral ground.[6] She picked that pepper grass then came over here to sell it to me to put in my gumbo. Now, I just buy the stuff.* Chicken, chaurice, smoked sausage, and veal stew meat are added to the soup. The heavy gumbo is the only thing on the menu on Holy Thursday, the restaurant is packed and a line stretches out the door and down the sidewalk. Practically every Creole in New Orleans is either seated inside or waiting for a table. As New Orleans attorney Bernard Charbonnet says, "You had to have grown up seeing your mother cut up those different herbs. You grew up with it. It's a cultural event. You won't miss it."

GUMBO DES HERBES

1 bunch mustard greens
1 bunch collard greens
1 bunch turnips
1 bunch watercress
1 bunch beet tops
1 bunch carrot tops
½ head lettuce
½ head cabbage
1 bunch spinach
2 medium onions, chopped
4 cloves garlic, mashed
   and chopped
Water

1 lb. smoked sausage
1 lb. smoked ham
1 lb. chaurice (hot)
1 lb. brisket stew meat
1 lb. boneless brisket
5 tbsp. flour
1 tsp. thyme leaves
1 tbsp. salt
1 tsp. cayenne pepper
1 tbsp. filé powder

Clean all vegetables, making sure to pick out bad leaves and rinse away all grit. In a large pot, place all greens, onions, and garlic. Cover with water and boil for 30 minutes. While this is boiling, cut all meats and sausages into bite-size pieces and set aside. Strain vegetables after boiling and reserve liquid. In a 12-quart stockpot place brisket meats, ham, smoked sausage, and 2 cups reserved liquid and steam for 15 minutes. While steaming, place chaurice in skillet and steam until chaurice is rendered (all grease cooked out). Drain chaurice, keeping the grease in the skillet, and set aside.

All vegetables must be puréed. This can be done in a food processor or by hand in a meat grinder. Heat the skillet of chaurice grease and stir in flour. Cook roux for 5 minutes or until flour is cooked (does not have to brown). Pour roux over meat mixture; stir well. Add vegetables and 2 quarts reserved liquid. Let simmer for 20 minutes. Add chaurice, thyme, salt, and cayenne pepper; stir well. Simmer for 40 minutes. Add filé powder; stir well and remove from heat. Serve over steamed rice. Yield: 8 servings.

The word *Creole* has come to embody many different meanings to different people. While Leah Chase's family stretches across the color spectrum, from black and dark-skinned to white, it remains distinctively Creole, just as it was when Leah was a girl growing up in Madisonville. What about the next generation? With Leah as family matriarch, one can believe the Creole cultural heritage will live on, but in her manner: less discriminatory but always Catholic.

CHAPTER ELEVEN

The Next Generation

It seems only normal to discuss Leah Chase with her grandchildren. After all, if there is to be a legacy to her story, they are it.

Her grandchildren pull no punches when asked about their grandmother. One memorable day, five of them gathered around a table in the Gold Room. At the time, Wayne Reese was twenty-two and his brother, Alfred, was ten; their cousin David Haydel was eighteen; Little Dooky (Edgar Chase IV) was seventeen; and Chase Kamata, the only girl in the group, was sixteen.

When asked, "What happens when your grandmother acts old fashioned?", they all jumped in at once:

"You can't talk back."

"She'll hit you or fuss at you."

"Strict discipline."

"If your opinion is different than hers, don't voice it."

"But that's okay; she's right most of the time."

David, one of Emily's sons, recalled a day he was taking her somewhere in his truck. When he passed through one busy intersection, she said, "You better slow down. One day, you're going to get in a wreck. I feel like we're going one hundred miles an hour in this little truck." She also advised her grandson to put on his seat belt. He told her he wasn't going to get in any wreck. A few days later, he passed through the same intersection. A guy ran a red light and wham! David's car was hit broadside.

"I had to tell her," he said. "But she never said, 'I told you so.' You never want to believe her when she's telling you something, but you learn . . . she's usually right."

Leah is profoundly close to her grandchildren, and the feeling is mutual. When Emily died, leaving a husband and seven children, Leah considered moving into her daughter's house. She felt they needed her and that she could help. Ultimately, she decided not to, but she called the children every single day when they got home from school, to be sure everything was okay.

Leah Kamata, Leah's youngest daughter, regards her mother's treatment of Emily's children as less stern than she should be: "She is more forgiving of their actions because they don't have a mother. She believes they missed out on a lot of nurturing and she has been committed to filling in."

Alva, Leah's daughter-in-law, credits the older woman with how well rounded Emily's children are: "She was there for them. She's done a tremendous job with Emily's kids. The little crew . . . to be so young and lose their mother, it was tough, real tough."

Chase, Leah Kamata's daughter, considers her and her grandmother as having a lot in common. "I sorta take after her. I like to do a lot of things and I tend to do them all at once. She fussed once that I was too involved and that I needed to spend more time with my family. 'Family is first,' she said. 'You never spend time with your family.'" Chase remembers being hurt. She loved her theater activities and she volunteered for a lot of things. She felt wrongly criticized. The issue boiled over into a big emotional scene and Chase says, "At first I resented it, but after she talked to me, I came around. She was right. I was wrong, as usual."

The grandchildren jump into each other's comments, each one remembering his or her own story. Alfred remembers going with his grandmother to the mall and asking to go to a toy store. "No, later," she said. He kept begging. "Stop that, little boy, before I hit you," she said. He kept begging. "Then," he said, "she just hit me. She bopped me in the kitchen one day because I was talking slang."

Quiet chuckles. The grandchildren love her, and they enjoy reminiscing about her. They know what it is that their grandmother absolutely will not accept.

Unanimously and in unison, they say: "Talking back. You cannot talk back to your parents, to elderly people. And **don't** walk away from her when she's talking to you! 'Don't walk away from me. I didn't tell you could leave. Stay right here.'"

When it comes to Leah's cooking, the grandchildren happily announce their favorites.

"We all go through our gumbo phase," explains Wayne, "but I'm in my jambalaya phase, right now."

"Crawfish étouffée and meatballs," declares Little Dooky.

"Gumbo and fried chicken," says Alfred, grinning. "She has the best gumbo."

"For me," says David, "shrimp Clemenceau."

When it's convenient, the grandchildren stop by the restaurant after school, make a sweep through the kitchen, serve themselves a plate of whatever is cooking, and settle down to eat. They know they're welcome.

CREOLE GUMBO

4 hard-shell crabs, cleaned
½ lb. Creole hot sausage,
   cut in bite-size pieces
½ lb. smoked sausage,
   cut in bite-size pieces
½ lb. boneless veal stew meat
½ lb. chicken gizzards
½ cup vegetable oil
4 tbsp. flour
1 cup onion, chopped
4 qt. water
6 chicken wings, cut in half

½ lb. chicken necks,
   skinned and cut
½ lb. smoked ham, cubed
1 lb. shrimp, peeled and
   deveined
1 tbsp. paprika
1 tsp. salt
3 cloves garlic, chopped fine
¼ cup parsley, chopped
1 tsp. ground thyme
24 oysters with their liquid
1 tbsp. filé powder

Put crabs, sausages, stew meat, and gizzards in 6-quart pot over medium heat. Cover and let cook in its own fat for 30 minutes (it will produce enough, but continue to watch the pot). Heat oil in skillet and add flour to make a roux. Stir constantly until very brown. Lower heat, add onions, and cook over low heat until onions wilt. Pour onion mixture over the ingredients in the large pot. Slowly add water, stirring constantly. Bring to a boil. Add chicken wings, necks, ham, shrimp, paprika, salt, garlic, parsley, and thyme. Let simmer for 30 minutes. Add oysters and liquid; cook for 10 minutes longer. Remove from heat; add filé powder, stirring well. Serve over rice. Yield: 8-10 servings.

Any new girlfriend or boyfriend must submit to a rite of passage with Grandmother. The grandchildren all confess to being nervous before presenting someone new to Leah. "She doesn't forget a thing," says David, "and the next day, she'll ask you, 'Well, why was she like this?' or 'Why did she say that?'

"Yeah, and she'll tell me, 'That girl's stupid; she's not the right girl for you,'" says Wayne.

In an age where people spend a fortune buying distressed jeans, which are sold as brand new, Leah threatens her grandchildren: "If I ever see you wearing jeans to school or coming here wearing jeans, I'll rip 'em off and tear them up." And to Wayne, who is a portly man who likes to wear his clothes loose, she constantly admonishes him, "Wayne, pull your pants up. Tuck your shirt in."

"She doesn't miss anything," smiles David. "She catches everything we do."

Leah's oldest grandchild, Tracie, firstborn of Emily, considers her relationship with her grandmother special:

> "[She is] not only my Grandmother but she has taken on the role of mother since my mother's passing. As if her plate wasn't already full, she helped raise my six other siblings and me. Grandmother has to be involved in everything and has to do everything, whether it is the restaurant, the community, or, most importantly, her family. [She] is the cornerstone of our family and makes sure we stay strong together as a family. Once a month, we had our Sunday breakfast and she made sure that everybody's favorite dish was on the table. But sometimes, she can't wait for her monthly head count. If she hasn't seen you or received a call from you at least once during the week, then you will get summoned. On several occasions, I was summoned. Grandmother didn't wait until you got home to call you. Wherever you were, that's where you got your summons. . . . When I was in nursing school, she called the school secretary and had her call me out of class just so she could tell me to come to the restaurant later on that day. Grandmother has to know what everyone is doing at all times, or else the gumbo won't come out right!

Leah counts on her grandchildren to help her. They drive her places, deliver things for her, pick her up, and lend a hand in the restaurant when called upon. One day, two groups of people were scheduled for dinner in the restaurant: fifty people in the Victorian

Room and fifteen in the Gold Room. It was Cleo's day off and the other sous-chef didn't show up. Travis, who waits tables in the restaurant, asked his grandmother what she was going to do. "I'll get that little rascal Dook here to help me plate up the food," she said, smiling fondly. "Dook" is what she calls Little Dooky.

As Travis went back and forth into the kitchen, he heard grandmother and grandson bickering together good naturedly.

"Dook, watch that stuffed shrimp, that you don't overcook it."

"Aren't you closer to it? You watch it," he laughed. This is the kind of retort that has earned Little Dooky the nickname, Smart Mouth. His sarcastic but humorous way of responding to the adults in the family when they ask him to do something amuses the other young people. And he gets away with it. His brothers think it's because he's the last of the Dookys, at least for now. And they observe that, while he lips off to everyone else, he never does to Grand-D, the name the kids use for their grandfather. "That must have something to do with Grand-D being head Dooky," notes Travis.

Not many eighty-year-old women have grandsons who go to college, get degrees, then come home to learn more from their grandmother, but Leah does. Travis Chase got his bachelor's degree in business and Japanese studies, then moved to Japan for a couple of years to participate in the Japan Exchange Teacher Program of the Consulate General of Japan. After working in business and advertising for a while, he asked his grandmother if he could work with her at the restaurant.

Unlike many of his cousins, he'd never waited a table in his life. His great fear was spilling everything on the clients or just not managing anything correctly. There was no training course to become a waiter at the Dooky Chase Restaurant. It was baptism by fire, *and* by Grandmother. "You learned by constant practice and countless errors with Grandmother whipping every waiter into shape until, finally, you could handle anything." When Leah saw her grandson do something wrong, she scolded him. And when he did something right, she complimented him. And she reminded him that at his age she was waiting on fifty or sixty people by herself, and handling it.

His grandmother's dedication and the amount of time and energy she is able to give to her work are examples to Travis. At twenty-three years old, he wonders how she does it all. Yet her passion for her work has left a firm imprint on the younger Chase. Travis plans to enter graduate school then return to the field of advertising, and he believes he will have the same passion for his future work that his grandmother has for hers. He knows her philosophy by heart: "Don't worry if you get knocked down in life, because that will happen. Just learn from that experience and keep moving."

Leah and Dooky Chase have fifteen grandchildren—sixteen, counting Nathan, who is deceased. They have eight great-grandchildren. While most of the young generation live around New Orleans, some live as far afield as Oregon, Georgia, and North Carolina, and some have lived overseas. When the out-of-towners are in New Orleans for any reason, they roam in and out of what they call "The Restaurant." It's the meeting place. They go by, knowing they'll eat. The gumbo for the body is only part of the menu. They know they'll also get a dose of gumbo for the soul—at least if their grandmother is in the kitchen.

Leah Chase naively walked into a family business over fifty years ago and, over the years, has transformed it into something that far surpasses a business. It is first and foremost a meeting place, and the Chase-Lange family members are the first to pull their chairs up to the tables. Close on the heels of the family are numerous groups—be they political, cultural, religious, or social—who have sat at Leah's tables and made prodigious decisions over Leah's food.

It is also a monument. To all the people who fought and won battles for civil rights, for voting rights, and for union rights in the city of New Orleans, the Dooky Chase Restaurant is a proud reminder that some rules must be broken to better humankind.

And it is an oasis. When black artists had no venue to exhibit their work, the walls of the Dooky Chase Restaurant, thanks to Leah Chase's interest, support, and love of beauty, became their gallery. And perhaps, this is the identification that most symbolizes the life of Leah Chase: art smoothes the edges. Beauty makes human beings see the world differently. And it was, after all, the

Impressionist painter Paul Gauguin who, in 1898, said, "All that matters in life is Where do we come from? What are we? Where are we going?"

He could well have been speaking about the Chase family.

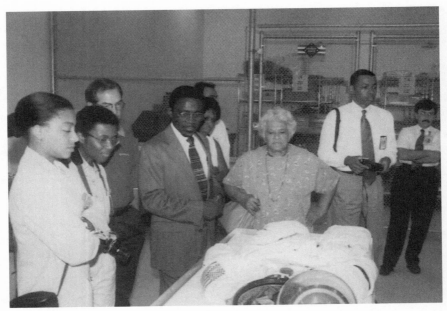

Leah Chase at Cape Canaveral Space Launch observing an astronaut uniform

CHAPTER TWELVE

Listen, I Say Like This

Leah wears a tee shirt that has 'Listen, I say like this.' emblazoned across its front. Actress Cicely Tyson gave it to her during the filming of the HBO movie, *A Lesson Before Dying*, based on the book written by Ernest Gaines. According to Leah, whenever old, Creole people wanted to make a point, they would say, "Listen, I say like this." The tee shirt is appropriate.

Leah Lange Chase is a lady with strong opinions—on everything. She has thousands of opportunities to say, 'Listen, I say like this.' Every time something newsworthy happens, someone from the media trots over to Leah to get her comments. She's a voice of the community. When John Glenn rocketed into space at the age of seventy-seven, a local television studio sent a representative to ask Leah what she thought about it. Little did the reporter know, Leah is an avid space fan, has been to two space launches at Cape Canaveral, knows several astronauts on a first-name basis, and wouldn't mind going up herself.

"Well, if he comes back with fewer wrinkles, I'm going next," she told the reporter. Sometimes Leah Chase says outrageous things, and sometimes she pays a heavy price for her comments, but she is never deterred from speaking her mind.

Her daughter, Stella, analyzes her mother this way: "My mother really does not put on. When you see my mother, it is always **my mother**. When you ask her something she tells you the truth, at least as she perceives the truth. She doesn't dress up her comments and she tells you regardless of your color. I think people respect what she says because they know they're going to hear exactly how she feels. She's herself."

Younger daughter, Leah, views her mother with a certain sense of humor: "I call her the Godfather, making sure everything is right. She needs to be involved. If anything happens to ANYONE, she'll say, 'You know, if I could have been there, I could have changed that.' [In her mind] everything, for some reason, comes back to her in some way. I tell her, 'Jesus was on the cross with two martyrs; should I put up another cross for you to be next to him?' Or I tell her, 'Oh, let me get another nail, Mother.' She has a need to help, to be involved. That's what makes her the person she is. She has this great caring."

The Prince, as young Leah calls her brother, Edgar, says, "When my mother speaks from the heart, she speaks well. She's funny, although she can be very pushy and very determined and stubborn. When she gets real busy, she can actually be offensive to some people. She'll call somebody a stupid jackass, *not* a flattering term."

Her priest, Father Mike, as she calls him, says, "She's always preaching. And she doesn't care who she's talking to. She's going to tell you what she believes. She'll tell you a story about a painting that is a Civil Rights thing, and then she tells the kids what they should be doing today. She commands by her presence: 'I'm here; you have to pay attention.'"

Dr. Andrea Jefferson, prominent New Orleans citizen and wife of U.S. Congressman William Jefferson, has known Leah Chase for a long time. "When Mrs. Chase speaks, people listen. She is one of the voices, not only of the black community, but of the community at large. A lot of early meetings are held at Dooky Chase's with Leah sitting in offering advice and giving counsel. When Pat Taylor was considering running for Congress, his first meeting was at Dooky Chase. He's a white Republican, Taylor Energy. He called together a network of black community leaders and community activists. . . . You may disagree with her on some political issues, but you can't be disagreeable when you disagree. She is a real lady, upright, lots of character, very moral. . . . She gives more of herself than most people give and she never asks anything in return. Never. She lives by this: do what you can to make the world a better place."

I'm a stickler for people doing what they're supposed to do in life.

Leah Chase receiving the Weiss Brotherhood Award (New Orleans chapter of the National Conference on Christians and Jews)

*When I see people who will do nothing . . . you will do **nothing** at all to better this world that you live in? I can't figure that one out. . . . If you think you're doing something right, then pass it on. I truly believe, whatever you do, you got to bring somebody with you. You can't go up that ladder by yourself. No indeed. If that rung breaks, you're down. If somebody's there, they can give you a hand. One man on the mountain ain't gonna work. . . . What makes me angry is when I see people not doing what they're really supposed to do. And they say, 'Oh, let it go,' and I say, 'No, I'm not going to let it go.' That's the trouble with people today. Everybody's letting it go. Don't tell me let it go, when I know you're wrong. I'm not going to do that. That causes me to lose my temper around here—bad news sometimes.*

Leah Chase has had, or at least has taken, many opportunities to say what she thinks about various community issues. Former Freedom Rider Dr. Rudy Lombard says, "There is nothing significant in the African-American community in New Orleans that Leah is not involved in." Indeed.

POLITICS

*When it's time for election, the mayor hits the streets. First place he hits? The Projects. All he wants 'em to do is go to that poll and vote what he says vote. That is wrong. You go to these people as often as you can. And you say, 'Man, let's try to get this together here. **We** living here.' That doesn't mean you have to get **down** to these people. 'I don't have to go in my old jeans. I'm going in my suit. I'm the mayor. I want you to know that. I'm your leader, and I'm going to try to lead you the right way. You have to do something to help me.' People would do that. I think you can do anything with people, except those . . . like my mother used to say, 'Don't waste your time there cause God can't even help 'em.' You just keep going. You do what you can to lift up everybody but you don't sit on your fanny and don't do anything.*

[Concerning the mayoral race in which Marc Morial ran against Donald Mintz:) As many people came and said ugly things, twice as many came and said, 'Leah, you're right. We're with you.' One commercial came out I thought was pretty neat. It said, 'We love you Leah but you're wrong this time.' That's the way it should be. If you think I'm wrong, you say I'm wrong. That's okay. That's the system. You do what you want; I'll do what I want. In the end we'll come together. . . . You don't vote for your friend because he's your friend. You don't vote for a man because he's black or he's white. You look at him. You look at his character. You vote for the man who you think is going to do the best for everybody. We don't need more registered voters. We need to educate the ones we have.

*He isn't going to owe you anything or be indebted to you. That's the way I feel about any politician I work for. You don't owe me anything. I am supporting you because I think you can do the best for **all** of us— everybody. Now, if you can get this city working for all of us, I'm going to do my share.*

*We should meet with our congressmen, with the people we send to Washington. Not all the time to talk about what they need to do, but just to let them know where we're coming from. Like I should invite my senator to dinner, and my representative. Then they'll know **me**. We should be closer to those people. They'll know what we're all about. I really believe that most people who go into politics, it's a sacrifice. They can make more money with less hassle outside.*

*You gonna have to have **some** gun control. You gonna have to put some laws down. And it's more than that little lock you're putting on there. That's hogwash. Take all the handguns off. Nobody needs rapid-firing shotguns. That has nothing to do with hunters. You need to take those others away. It is out of hand. . . . Look at who you've got with guns. They can't shoot! These people you're giving guns . . . a bunch of dummies who can't think their way out of a paper bag. And they can't shoot. They were not trained to shoot.*

Some politicians tell the people, 'Look, you gotta do this because you're black.' I say, don't go that way. Don't do this. Don't come to this restaurant because I'm black. Come because I can give you some kind of service. That makes me a bad business person if you come here just because I'm black. You come because 'I know Leah is going to give me service when I get there; I know I can tell Leah what I want; I know Leah is going to give me something for my money.' That's why you come here.

SCHOOLS

You should not have allowed those magnet schools the way you did.[1] I'm dead against those schools. They take all the money and all the best kids. That's not fair to that other poor little child who can barely make a C. If you left some people there to help and inspire him, maybe he would feel good about that. I think they were created [by people] who are kinda elitist. They can say they have some little children from the projects. Well, I bet you can count them on your fingers. Some of the doctors, and all that, I have to say, 'Okay, you can pay tuition. You can pay to send your child to Ursuline or some other private school. Pay! Give somebody else a chance who can't pay.' They're dumping all the money in the schools for the children who can pay, and the children who can't pay, they are just left out.

*Accountability is **the** thing. If you don't make people accountable for the job they're doing, they're not going to do it. When you get in office, you say, 'These are my goals. This is what we're going to try to reach— at all costs. It might get somebody blown away here, but we're going to reach this goal.' And that's what you have to do. I'm gonna hurt somebody in the meantime. That's all right, too, but we're going to get the goal. People go at things too much as one person. It's not about you; it's not about me. It's about the whole system. You **got** to do the big thing. And* *that's what people don't want to do. Somebody's always going to get hurt along the way, and that's the name of the game. . . . Now, if I'd been working on the school board for a hundred years and nothing changed, what should I do? Get off! Get off and give somebody else a chance.*

See that they [children] have a nice space to go to school, and tell the teachers: 'Look, I'm not telling you how to dress here, but please, these children come from low-income families and poor mama doesn't have anything.' That teacher is an inspiration. Can't she look pretty? Can't she look nice? Some of the teachers look awful. I remember telling a little teacher (Stella was at that school and she told me, 'Oh Mother, you can't say that.' And I said, 'I can and I will.'), 'You cannot do that. You cannot come to this school with these fringe-on-the-bottom jeans and no stockings on and some kind of tee shirt with something on it. Uh-uh. You can't do that. Not for these children, you can't.'

*No. It's proper behavior for everybody. The rule is for everybody. If I say you can't come to school with your hair stacked a mile high, you can be green. But you can't come to school with your hair . . . That's what it's all about. That's what you do when you go to parties. That's your party attire. We are training you to fit this world, the business world, where you have to work. And that's what you got to do. . . . But we got to the place where you can't tell anybody anything for fear they'll get offended. I truly believe a principal can call the parents together and tell them, 'Listen, I'm going to teach your children. I'm going to take good care of your children. I **need** your help.' Not 'You **must** do this,' no. 'I need your help.'*

*You know, a lot of black legislators didn't like that [bill] at all.[2] I don't have any problem with that. **You're** sitting up there; you didn't have the guts to say we want this for our children. Here comes this man and does it. Hey, that's good for me. What are you going to do? Because you didn't think of it, you didn't have the guts to say we want this for our children. It's good. It's good. One man said, 'That program is not good because our children can't pass the test. . . .' Stop right there! You cannot tell children what they **can't** do. They **can** pass this test. We're the only race of people who tell their children they can't. They **can.***

COMMUNITY DEVELOPMENT
Now the World's Fair [World Exposition 1984] . . . the way I look at

*it, it was very good. I went to the meeting in Paris with Dutch. I heard the man who was the secretary of the thing say, 'You're not going to make money.' He said, 'It's not to make money. It's to show what you have to the rest of the world.' But that wasn't told to people. I thought we should have had this big meeting in the city, and we'd all work together and say, 'We're selling our city.' And that's it. All the carpenters there are in this city? We'd get all the black carpenters in the city and tell them, 'You can show us off here. You come do this.' We'd get residual benefits out of it. We got a lot. We got those buildings that were just old tumbled-down warehouses. We got new sidewalks. . . . The president of the country should always open the World's Fair. You're selling **your** country.*

You make your neighborhood what you want it to be. I insist that you make your own neighborhood. Running away from it isn't going to help anything or anybody. You can do your part to uplift people. I think you should build things up and I battle that every day. This little bit of remodeling and decoration you see here was something nobody but my own little eye could see. I think you owe people something. If you do things worthy of the people, then people will do differently. They will act differently. I think when you're in business you have to look at life this way—it's about taking a risk. If you can't take a risk, you shouldn't be in business. I say like this, if you can't take a risk, you're wasting God's good time on this earth.

You haven't shown me enough of all the money you say is there [federal housing]. I don't want to hear that you're sending money back. I don't want to hear that. The goody-two-shoes days are over. That's what I told Dooky. He said, 'Honey, you be a nice lady.' And I told him, 'I lived to the year 2000 and I'm not going to be a nice lady anymore—end of the nice lady stuff.'

SOCIAL JUSTICE

When I went to St. Mary's Academy and we had to say the Pledge of Allegiance to the flag, when it got to one part, 'with liberty and justice for all,' I wouldn't say it. My daddy used to say, 'Don't rumple the waters. Don't do that.' But I wouldn't say it. It wasn't true!

I can remember when we had to register little babies in Madisonville. We had to register the babies at the house of a lady across the street from us, and she took the papers to Covington. When my little sister was born, I registered her. I don't think I was in high school yet. I wouldn't put Colored. I put Negro. My daddy was upset. He said, 'No, you just making trouble. You put Colored.' And I said, 'No, we're not colored; we're Negro.' . . . Then it came along and we were not going to be Negroes anymore; we wanted to be referred to as black. 'Okay,' I said, 'doesn't matter to me, I'm black. I'll do that. Negro is black.' Then we didn't want to be black anymore. We were going to be African-Americans. . . . 'Stop right there. I stop at black. This is it. I'm not going any further.' What you call me doesn't make me any different than what I am. Those kind of little things that I didn't like, you know. I didn't raise a fuss about it. In my mind, I just didn't like it.

I didn't like to sit behind that [segregated] bus thing. Why? I remember how stupid it looked to me. Here was this little piece of wood eight inches high, separating me from you. That was stupid. I could see if you had a wall where you couldn't see me and I couldn't see you, but this little piece of wood? I just felt like pitching it away because it looked absolutely stupid to me. So you know what I used to do? The sign said nothing on one side and on the other side it said, Colored. So I'd take it out and put it in the wrong way.

When Dr. Martin Luther King, Jr., died, I refused to put a black wreath on my door. Nobody needed to intimidate me. I was just as sorry as you were that Martin was dead, but you can't tell me to do things like that and intimidate me. I didn't like things like that. I never liked things like that. If people were not sorry King was dead, that's their problem. If they were sorry, okay. . . . Putting the black thing on the door wouldn't help anything.

In the Civil Rights movement, you had some people jumping on the bandwagon who did the wrong things, because they don't have it all up here [tapping on her head], or they don't have enough smarts to think things out, so they just get on the band wagon. They have some purpose, some good, so you don't turn them away. You put up with them. That happens in all movements everywhere. I remember when Pope John XXIII (Vatican II) changed the whole church. One bishop said, 'That's good, the changes. But what he doesn't understand, he's opening all the windows to let in the fresh air. But there will be some birds fly in and mess up the

Leah Chase and Bryant Gumble

whole place.' Which is true. That happens with everything. But those are the chances you take in life. Sometimes if you didn't have that kind of person, you wouldn't have any movement at all.

They have a real clique there in that Boston Club, the Rex people, and so forth.[3] You got to be the Pope to get in the Boston Club. I don't have a problem with that. That's your business. I can't afford to be there. If that's what they want to do with their money—dues, Mardi Gras parades, etc.—in my opinion, that's antiquated. But if that's what you like to spend your money on, go ahead. That's not important to me. You can have your little old club all by yourself; I don't care. Some people get offended but I don't care. But those people do their part in the community. They're the biggest contributors to Mardi Gras and all that. I just don't have time. I'm too busy trying to get myself where I'm supposed to be. There are other things to think about. We need to get these schools working.

SOCIETY AS A WHOLE

*Those songs are terrible. The words that people are allowed to use, terrible, wrong. You don't do that. On one end, you're talking about not destroying the environment. Well, my God, you're spitting out all this stuff from your mouth. You're hurting my ears with it. That's bad news. We just have to put a stop to it. People have to stop saying, 'Well, that's just today.' It's **not** today. It's what you're allowing today.*

*Tipper Gore was right to attack rap music. The industry should be stopped. You got to tell people nicely, 'I don't like what you're doing. That doesn't mean I don't like **you**. I don't like what you're doing; it's wrong.' You can tell the parent to turn the television off but the child is going to hear it on the street. When Blue Lu Barker put out her song, **that** was wrong.[4] She had this piece, 'Don't you feel my legs/ if you feel my legs you're going to feel my thighs/ and if you feel my thighs you're going to go up high . . .' That was bad lyrics. You inferred bad things. So Franklin Roosevelt said, 'Look, I'm not playing that for my soldiers. You're not playing this for my soldiers. That's it.' So that was it. So Blue Lu goes to something else. She was talented you know. She could go for something else and be just as famous.*

Look at Eva Perón. I like the struggle that girl had. She came from

Leah Chase and Quincy Jones

nowhere, made a mistake. When she got to the top, she proceeded to mash the people at the top. No. You go with them. You get them to join you. You don't knock them down. Did you get there just to knock somebody down? Uh-uh. That was a grave mistake she made, poor darlin', as sick as she was. She was gonna step on all the rich people. You don't do that. You not gonna bring up the poor by stepping on the rich people—mistake.

*Dr. Kevorkian . . . if abortion is okay—you tell this woman she can abort this human being; it has two legs, two arms, a head, and you can throw it in the garbage can—why can't **he** kill somebody? So you just have to make the rules. You can break them. I can't keep you from breaking them, but I can certainly tell you it's wrong. You can't do that.*

FAMILY AND CHILDREN

When John Kennedy, Jr., crashed, you think about all kinds of things. Poor Rose. That's the first thing I thought about. This boy goes down in that water, and that had to be horrible. This child had to be disoriented. Can you imagine? You're flying around in the darkness, you don't know where you are, you don't know what to do, your plane is dropping a mile a minute, and here you are, helpless. It must have been awful for him. . . . This family has given a lot, and look what has happened to them, and they keep going. Where do they get their faith from? Looks like God keeps slapping them down and they keep coming back. Their faith is unbelievable. It's good to have that faith, when you think about it. You just put yourself in God's hands and say, 'Hey, it's up to you.'

*Adults are not acting like adults today. The biggest mistake that's being done all over today . . . adults are putting children on their level. That is a terrible mistake. Parents are afraid of the children and afraid to hurt the children. They're afraid the children won't like **them** for some reason.*

We're not telling people what's wrong. If it's wrong, I'm going to tell you it's wrong. I don't tell you it's wrong by what I think; just look at the rules that were laid down for man, whether it's the Ten Commandments or the laws of the land. You're doing this against the rule. You're wrong! I tell that to children all the time.

One girl working for me came to talk to me about her mother who was on drugs. I said, 'Look at the fourth commandment.' It says 'Honor your father and your mother, period.' If your mother is in the gutter, she's your mother. Her problem is her problem, not yours. If you disrespect her, you answer for it. She answers for her mistakes. Your life is harder than the next one, okay, but you have to remember that's your mother.'

You hear, 'I raped so-and-so because my daddy beat me or something.' Hey! Wrong! You got a responsibility to yourself. I don't care what your daddy did. That's his problem. Everybody is shifting the blame. It is frightening. You have to just take a stand and tell people. And I think you can tell them in a way that you don't offend them. You just tell them what you don't like.

It's harder for children today. My children . . . I wasn't the information desk, no: 'Just do what I tell you to do and keep doing it.' But today, you cannot do that. You have to talk to them just to make them understand where you're coming from.

Any time your child does something wrong, it hurts you. It's painful to you. You as a parent think it's something you did wrong. You just have to talk to them and keep talking and keep talking. But you have to remember one thing, just because they're your children, they're not flawless. They're children. They'll do just what the others do. Children are exposed to so much. They go with this one; they see that one do something; they do the same thing. You have to keep talking, keep talking. Sometimes you have to talk downright ugly to them. But keep talking.

People say, 'You know, you can give your children too much.' I don't think so. You can't give children too much when it comes to material things. The only thing happens there is if you don't give them enough of yourself. There are no bad children. Look at that parent. Once in a while, you see good parents lose a child, you know, fall off the track a bit. But look back to that parent. Parent got selfish, parent got to thinking only about himself.

You have to give up your life for your children, so don't go around here just getting children and not marrying. When you bring those children in the world, you're responsible—just one piece of clay. You've got to mold it. You've got to make it. When children turn out to be whatever they are, the parents can be proud. They didn't do that on their own. It took that mama, more than that daddy. It took that mama.

Stories of Leah's involvement in the lives of her own children and grandchildren are legendary. Her daughter-in-law recalls when her twin boys were seventeen and went somewhere with friends: "I didn't want them to go and their daddy let them go. I was mad at them and I was mad at him. I had to pick up Mother-in-law (what the spouses of Leah's children call her) and take her to my house and I was fussing and fussing about the twins. Mother-in-law just took it in. She didn't say a word, just listened. Finally, when the twins came home, she went in their bedroom and just punched them out. She told them, 'You're not going to get my son in any trouble.' And she punched them. She's very territorial about her children. She's always telling the grandchildren 'You're not going to hurt my kids,' or 'Don't you worry your mother.'"

When one of Leah's grandsons upset his parents, Leah disapproved of how the parents reprimanded him. *I'd take him and punch the heck out of him. 'Look, you hurt your mama. You did this wrong thing. If I ever catch you by yourself, you got it coming. I'll beat the heck out of you.'*

One day, a little girl was hanging all over my grandson, you know, in those little bobtail dresses they wear? I said, 'Back off, back off.' And they said, 'Grandmother, you can't tell that to that girl.' I said, 'Look, back off, because I'm telling you, if you come up with a baby, he's not gonna marry you.' My grandson said, 'Grandmother, how could you tell her that?' I said, 'I don't know, but I just did.' Those little girls . . . you got to keep talking to them.

One of my granddaughters had a doozy of a boyfriend. She put him down for some other stupid somebody. I said, 'Let me talk to you girl. Let me talk to you straight.' I said, 'Listen to me well. You can look at all this baloney this other guy is telling you, and all this glamour and all this big smile. You can't eat it, and as my mother said, you can't spend it on Canal Street. So don't fall for none of that junk.' I said, 'Listen, you can learn to love a gorilla if he treats you well enough.' 'Oh Gram!' she says. 'I'm telling you. I'm telling you.'

Sometimes my grandkids say, 'Don't come around Gram. Don't bring your girlfriend around Grandmother because she's gonna level with them.' But you have to keep on them. Sometimes I see faltering I don't like and I have to call them on the side. I never tell the mother I'm doing that. Cause you know, people don't like that, even when it's your own children. Sometimes they think you're crazy and old, but you have to talk to them so hard today.

People say, 'But you beat your children.' They look at me and they think, 'She's awful; she's cruel.' I did whip them. And I mean I whipped them. But I never cursed them—not one time, not ever. And I defied anybody [who'd] curse my children. Don't do that. Because what you say horrible to a child, they never forget it. That little bruise will heal. They'll never feel that strap mark again, but those words will never go away.

My little grandson was at the back of my kitchen and he said, 'Oh, I'm bad.' Boom! I just gave it to him. 'Mercy!' he said. 'I'll never say that again.' I hate those slang words. And I just hit him so fast it shocked the daylights out of him. Used to be I didn't want to hear 'okay.' The word is 'all right.' My parents never let us use slang.

You want to give everything to your children, everything you didn't have. Sometimes they didn't even want what I wanted them to have: school bags, galoshes, and rain coats. My children hated that stuff. But I never had a school bag or galoshes or a raincoat. They hated it but they didn't say anything. Children were different then. They didn't have any choice. I didn't give them a choice. I didn't give them a choice of schools. I didn't give them a choice of anything.

Ever the champion for women, Leah nevertheless declares herself not a feminist. *I'm not a flag-waving person for women's rights. I believe women were created different for a purpose, in the eyes of God. I believe He put us above men and we should stay on that level. That's not to say we can't be whatever we want to be. We can be a politician or whatever. But if you want to do those kinds of things, I still think you have to remember you're a woman and you have to do the woman's things, too. And I think women can do that. I think they're capable. And most of them are doing that. I really do think women can do anything they set out to do. But like this war thing, women going in the war to fight? Look, I'll go in the army in a minute. I don't mind that. But when it comes to fighting that war, that's your job, man. You go. I'm not doing that. I think a woman can command a space rocket. But no matter what you do—you're on a rocket with these men—you have to remember you're a woman. Don't forget that. You don't have to use four-letter words with them and they don't have to with you. I really believe that. Women are special people and they should act like that. They could run the whole world and still act like a woman.*

I think a woman could be president of this country. I don't think a woman with little baby children would make a good president because she'd have to shift gears too many times. But I think a mature woman could be a good president. I think a woman can be good at anything she wants to be. And still be that woman, that wife, the lover of her husband. Now, a female can't, but a woman can. You're born a female; you become a woman. You have to look like a girl, act like a lady, think like a man, and work like a dog.

When I was a child, I wanted to be an altar girl. Not to serve God, but because I could talk Latin better than the boys. I just wanted to prove a point. But as you grow, you say, 'Now wait, I don't need to do that. I'm a girl. I'm a woman. I can be above that.' The older I get, the more I believe

*God created woman as a special person. Look at the biological differences. We are better, in plenty of things. When the boys here say, 'Miss Chase, you always calling us stupid.' I say, 'Because you are stupid. Men are stupid.' Just take Mr. Clinton, for instance. That was stupid action. [Monica Lewinsky affair] A woman would have **never** done that. Never. But his biological build got him aroused and got him in stupid trouble. That's the way he's built. I'm not built that way. It isn't that he's a dummy. My God, he's a Rhodes Scholar. He's brainy. But when push comes to shove . . . I am a woman. I can melt you. I can do whatever I want to you, when I want to. So that puts me on another level. I know I'm kind of biased but I believe that.*

I truly believe God must have a special space for women. Otherwise, if He's a 'just' God, like we believe, would he make us have to bear these children? These or things he put on women. We're to educate these children. We're to do everything for these children. I believe that if women live right, truly, there are special places [in Heaven] for women.

The women in the I Dream A World Exhibition . . . look at these two women from Mississippi. They couldn't send those men out there to make these voting rights happen, because the men would have been killed. So they went themselves. They just got up one morning, said their prayers, and went down to those voting polls. 'We're going to do what we have to do.' That's women. You don't have to make a lot of noise to do what you have to do. That's what women are all about.

The women today upset me. They upset me because they don't know their role as women. Emotionally, they are stronger than men. They may cry, but crying to me never denotes weakness. I cry every day—every single day. But I can dry those tears up and keep moving or I can let those tears flow and keep moving. That's what you're supposed to do. Women have to carry themselves like the great people they are. I tell them, 'You see, men are stupid. You are not stupid. Men were born stupid.'

Women have forgotten who they are. Women were given the job to create a human being in their bodies. That's a special thing. . . . I think you can be anything you want to be, but first you're a woman. You're special. You're different. You are different than that man and you better know it.

Epilogue

One July day in 1999, the heat index at the Lakefront Airport in New Orleans registered 106 degrees, and Leah Chase was in her kitchen cooking. There is no air conditioning in the kitchen and no big door to set ajar and let in a breeze. In fact, letting in any air at all are only two small jalousie windows: one in the dishwashing section and one in the cooking area. It's a sweatshop. When I asked her, "How do you do it?", I could have predicted her answer: "You do what you have to do."

The stove in Leah's kitchen has been there since the 1950s. A huge double sink with a spray hose dominates the dishwashing section. Years and years of souvenirs are tacked and taped to her cabinet doors. Drawers overflow with notebooks and notepads, scraps of paper with messages written on them, calendars, printed recipes, and any number of other once-important items. A rather worn-for-wear portable television sits on a table and is tuned to whatever program Leah and Cleo happen to want to listen to, and occasionally watch, as they work.

One reads about great chefs today and how they were trained. Inevitably, we learn a great chef "went through the hoops," so to speak. She or he worked in "all the stations" in one or more great restaurants, was sous-chef to some celebrated chef, attended a reputable cooking school, like Cordon Bleu in Paris or the French Culinary Institute in New York. Standing in Leah's kitchen and observing the activity going on makes the image of classical training for chefs seem ludicrous.

There may be fourteen stations in Leah's kitchen, but she and Cleo staff them all. Leah's training was acquired on her feet. She

Family portrait: Edgar Chase II, Stella Chase Reese, Leah Chase Kamata, Leah Chase, and Edgar Chase III

Leah with niece and sous-chef, Cleo Robinson

learned by doing, and the full responsibility of turning out good food rested squarely on her shoulders. She never had the benefit of training first and running her kitchen later. Everything happened simultaneously. Her school consisted of her memory of family cooking, observing others around her, having a new idea and trying it, taking risks, reading—and practice. Practice, practice, practice.

Yet few chefs in America can claim to have accomplished the things Leah has accomplished, or to have been described so lovingly and personally by her clients. People hear about her and her restaurant and they go, but they go for two reasons: first, they want to eat her Creole food, which is second to none in the city of New Orleans; and second, they hope to meet her, this unique woman who touches everyone she meets in a profound and long-lasting way.

Every year since 1985, Leah Chase has been honored by someone or some group for her service. Artists call her "Mother Chase." In February 1998, the *New Orleans Tribune* called her the "Sweetheart of New Orleans." Food critic Gene Bourg wrote in his June 27, 1990, *New York Times* column: "It's the kind of food that makes you want to run in the kitchen and hug the cook." Trumpeter and composer Hannibal Lokumbe wrote a work entitled "Gumbo a la Freedom: The Spices of Leah Chase," performed by the Louisiana Philharmonic Orchestra in March 2002. And John Folse, nationally known Cajun chef, pronounces her "the greatest Creole chef in New Orleans."

Face to face with Leah Chase, one senses right away that he or she is in front of *somebody*. This realization makes one reflect but also gives one confidence. Leah Chase's optimism and hope, undergirded by her faith, makes one leave her inspired, more light-hearted, more determined, and more thoughtful. Do other celebrity chefs have this effect on their clientele?

Now the Dooky Chase Restaurant has entered the twenty-first century. Some things need to change, but some things need to stay just the way they are. The things that need changing are trivial— the carpet in the dining room needs to be replaced, some new equipment needs to be put in the kitchens, the 1984 renovation needs sprucing up a bit. And Leah knows that better than anyone. A more modern organization needs to be put in place. The bar

Leah with Chef John Folse

needs a face-lift. And most important of all, more help is needed in the kitchen. Leah needs a break.

But the menu should never change. Nowhere in the city of New Orleans can a person find the Creole cuisine found at the Dooky Chase Restaurant. Many clients go to Leah's, and only to Leah's, to get their favorites. The name of the restaurant should never change. The location should never change. The ambiance should never change, and for sure, Leah can never leave.

She should just change places and move out front. She's spent her adult life in the kitchen, occasionally wandering into the dining rooms, much to the pleasure of her guests. It's time that's where she stayed. She should do as her mother-in-law did: Miss Emily was always out with the guests.

Happily, Leah has any number of grandchildren who could take over the business and maybe that's what will happen. But when young people come in, the older generation has to step aside. Young folks want to do things their way. If they're smart and patient, they'll ask questions of the older generation and follow advice when it's sound. But every family who has ever had a family business accepts one truth: there can be only one chief. Generally, when a younger generation takes over, they want to run the show themselves.

Leah Chase is not about to fold up her apron, set aside her baseball cap, and quit. She kicked off the year 2002 by preparing two thousand miniature new potatoes stuffed with an oyster filling for a charitable fundraiser: Chef's Charity for Children. Her cooking demonstration was before one thousand people, the day after her seventy-ninth birthday. These kinds of events are "quintessential Leah." The ideal life for her would be to have one foot in the restaurant—the restaurant that has come to be associated with her, her cooking and her personality—and the other foot outside, where she can still do the good things she is known for.

People who know and work with Leah Chase probably scratch their heads in wonder. One woman of simple and modest origins, self-taught as a chef, working with one assistant in an adequately equipped but certainly not state-of-the-art kitchen has systematically, for a half-century, nurtured individuals, families, colleagues, her city, and national movements. She has done this at her table,

Leah Chase (center), *daughters Stella and Leah* (center behind Leah), *and granddaughters*

with her cuisine and her presence: blunt, optimistic, and deeply caring.

She is a woman who has a lot to say, a woman with a lot of good sense, a woman who is not afraid to take a position. The rest of society will be well served if Leah Chase is able to do more than spend her days, 7:00 A.M. to midnight, in that kitchen, still cooking.

Appendix

LEAH CHASE'S
AWARDS AND ACHIEVEMENTS

2001 Honorary Doctorate of Education, Madonna College, Lavonia, Michigan

2001 Distinguished Hospitality Student Award, Penn College of Technology (scholarship given in her name)

2000 Southern Foodways Alliance Lifetime Achievement Award in Oxford Mississippi

2000 Ella Brennan *Savoire Faire* Award for Excellence, American Federation of Chefs (Louisiana chapter)

2000 Louisiana Gold Culinary Classic in Morial Convention Center in New Orleans

2000 Queen Cochon, Krewe of Pork and Beads, Cochon Cotillion by ABC 26 Children First

2000 Lafcadio Hearn Award, Nichols State University, Chef John Folse Culinary Institute

2000 Humanitarian Award, Holy Cross College

1999 Urban League Golden Gala Award: Community Service

1999 Amistad Patronage of the Arts Award

1998 Top Ladies of Distinction Community Service Award

1998 Spirit of the Dream Award, House of Blues Foundation

1997 *New Orleans Times-Picayune* Loving Cup

1997 Outstanding Woman Award, National Council of Negro Women

1996 University of New Orleans Entrepreneurship Award

1993 One of America's Top Black Chefs, 1,000 Black Men of Sonoma County

1992 Weiss Award from National Conference of Christians and Jews

1991 A. P. Tureaud Medal, State NAACP

1990 NAACP Human Understanding Award

1989 Included in *I Dream a World: Portraits of Black Women Who Changed America*

1989 Torch of Liberty Award, Anti-Defamation League of B'nai B'rith

1989 Anti-Defamation League's Torch of Liberty Award

1988 Outstanding Volunteer, Institute for Human Understanding, founded in 1952 by New Orleans Psychoanalyst, Dr. T. A. Waters

1988 Beautiful Activist Award

1987 Young Leadership Council Role Model Award

1986 Women in the Forefront Award

1985 Mayor's Arts Award

1985 Freedom Foundation Award

1984 Candace Award: Coalition of 100 Black Women

OTHER ACCOMPLISHMENTS

2002 *Gumbo a la Freedom* Hannibal Lokumbe, composer, orchestral piece commissioned in honor of Leah Chase.

2000 *Creole Cooking with Leah Chase* (television show)

1998 Taped segment for the *Today* show with Bryant Gumble

1995 Participated in Distinguished Chef Program, Nichols State University

1995 Taped *Cooking with Master Chefs* with Julia Child, also included in companion cookbook of the series

1995 Taped segment of *Plantation Cooking* with John Folse

1995 Taped segment of *Cooking with Alec Gifford*

CHASE FAMILY

Leah and Edgar Chase II

I. **Emily** (deceased) and James Haydel	II. **Stella** and Wayne Reese	III. **Edgar** and Alva Chase III	IV. **Leah Chase Kamata**
James and Leslie Haydel III	*Kimberly Reese*	*Trevor* and Minaxi Chase	*Chase Yuri*
James IV*	*Wayne Reese*	Ava*	
Nicholas*	*Myla Reese*	*Travis* and Chastity Chase	
Victor and Diedra Haydel	*Alfred Reese*	Caitlin*	
Emily*		Zoe*	
Victor II*		*Edgar* Chase IV (Little Dooky)	
Tracie and Michael Griffin			
Chase and Nia Haydel			
Isis*			
David Haydel			
Eve Haydel			
Robert Haydel			
Nathan (deceased)			

Legend

Bold Names—Leah's children
Italicized Names—Leah's grandchildren
*—Leah's great-grandchildren

Notes

CHAPTER 1

1. Roger Baudier, *The Catholic Church in Louisiana* (New Orleans: Imprimatur, 1939). St. Catherine's Church was constructed in 1919, with money donated by the Dendinger family, and placed under the patronage of St. Catherine of Alexandria in memory of Mrs. Catherine Dendinger, wife of Theodore Dendinger, Sr. (Mr. Dendinger was the owner of the Madisonville Saw and Planning Mill and a big donor to the town and to the Catholic church. The Dendinger family gave the building for the new church and the parishioners supplied the pews and altars.) The (older) St. Francis Xavier was turned over to the Negro Catholics of the community.

Two parochial schools were established before this: St. Catherine's school for white children began in 1916 under the Sisters of the Most Holy Sacrament, and the school for colored children was built in 1902 and staffed by the Sisters of the Holy Family.

2. *Chaurice* is a sausage that some think is similar to Spanish *chorizo* but varies in its ingredients from chef to chef and butcher to butcher. Leah Chase has used the *chaurice* made at Vaucresson, a family business that began in 1989, for more than forty years.

Several variations of gumbo exist. Filé gumbo, okra gumbo, and Creole gumbo are better known. Leah's Creole gumbo is a thick dark soup based on a roux (flour cooked in oil to a rich brown color) and includes crabs, sausage, chaurice, beef, ham, shrimp, oysters, and chicken, served over rice.

CHAPTER 2

1. A po' boy is a sandwich made of French bread that is sliced

down the middle and filled with dressing and any kind of meat or fried seafood.

CHAPTER 3

1.   Federal Writers' Project of the WPA, *New Orleans City Guide, American Guide Series* (Boston: Houghton Mifflin Company, 1938). The Municipal Auditorium, of Italian Renaissance architecture, is located at 727 St. Claude Avenue and was dedicated May 30, 1930, as a memorial to the dead heroes of the first World War.

2.   The Frontier Club was a social club of the same order of the Bunch Club, the Illinois Club, and other organizations within the black community that provided assistance to social causes within the city.

3.   See note 4 chapter 6. New Orleans is the only city in the United States that uses the term "neutral ground" for any street with a median. The first neutral ground was Canal Street. It was a boundary of sorts between the feuding Creoles in the old town and the Americans Uptown (Faubourg St. Mary). The wide median symbolized a truce that existed between the hostile residents of the two communities. In time, all medians in New Orleans came to be called "neutral grounds."

CHAPTER 4

1.   Available from www.blackbaseball.com/teams/grays1938.htm. Josh Gibson joined the Homestead Grays of the Negro National League in 1937 and, with first baseman Buck Leonard, "formed a power tandem called the black Babe Ruth and Lou Gherig" and dubbed the "Thunder Twins" by the press. They were referred to as the "Gashouse Gang" because their approach was considered close to that of the St. Louis Cardinals.

2.   Joe Louis, born May 13, 1914, began boxing professionally in 1934. He was known to many as the Brown Bomber and captured the heavyweight title of the world in 1937 against defending champion James J. Braddock in Chicago, a title he maintained for twelve years.

Beau Jack, born April 1, 1921, became a pro boxer in 1940 and captured the New York State Lightweight Title in 1942, which he kept until losing to Bob Montgomery in May 1943. Montgomery, known as the Philadelphia Bobcat, and born February 10, 1919, turned pro in 1938. Jack and Montgomery fought on August 4,

1944, in a nontitle bout at Madison Square Garden to a crowd of 15,822 spectators who generated a record gate (reported to be $35,864,000) that went toward war bonds.

3. Filé is powdered sassafras leaves used in cooking.

4. John Michael Vlach, "Sources of the Shotgun House: African and Caribbean Antecedents for Afro-American Architecture" (Ph.D. diss., Indiana University, 1975), 29, 31, 46. The shotgun house is a one room wide, one story high dwelling with two or more rooms, oriented perpendicularly to the road with its front door in the gable end. Traditionally, the interior doors of the house are aligned perpendicularly with the front and back doors, giving rise to the tale that one "can shoot a shotgun through the front door without doing any damage" because the doors are all in a line.

A double shotgun is simply two rooms wide, but incorporates the same layout of rooms and same placement of doors. Two shotguns can be built side by side, under one roof, to form a double shotgun.

5. Arnold R. Hirsh and Joseph Logsdon, "Simply a Matter of Black and White: The Transformation of Race and Politics in Twentieth Century," in *Creole New Orleans: Race and Americanization* (Baton Rouge: Louisiana State University Press, 1992).

New Orleans Times-Picayune, November 16, 2000. Donald Mintz: a Jewish attorney, civic leader, and community activist who ran for mayor twice: against Sidney Barthelemy in 1990 and against Marc Morial in 1994.

Sidney Barthelemy: a key leader of COUP (Community Organization for Urban Politics) and City Council member who first won the mayor's race in 1986 with twenty-five percent of the black vote and eighty-five percent of the white vote.

Dutch Morial: Mayor of New Orleans from 1978 to 1986.

Michael Bagneris: a local attorney and civic leader who served for six years as executive counsel for Mayor Dutch Morial and assumed the position of chief judge of Orleans Parish Civil District Court on January 1, 2001.

6. Brian Lanker, *I Dream A World: Portraits of Black Women Who Changed America* (New York City: Steward, Tabori and Chang, 1989).

CHAPTER 5

1. Department of the Army, New Orleans District, Corps of Engineers, *Hurricane Betsy, After-Action Report,* 1965, 5.

2. Ibid., 70.

3. *Betsy, American Red Cross Disaster Action,* September 1965.

4. Grillades: Leah's recipe is based on veal round steaks cooked in brown tomato gravy, seasoned with onion, garlic, celery, tomato, thyme, and parsley.

5. James Gill, *Lords of Misrule, Mardi Gras and the Politics of Race in New Orleans* (Jackson: University Press of Mississippi, 1997). For more information, see Henri Schindler, *Mardi Gras New Orleans* (New York: Flammarion, 1997).The Original Illinois Club was formed in 1895 under the leadership of Wiley Knight and quickly became the black Creole version of established white men's clubs that organized Carnival cotillions with mock royal courts and debutante balls.

Available from www.tulane.edu/~so-inst/divided25.html. The Southern Christian Leadership Conference (SCLC) resulted from a decision of eleven Southern ministers to formalize the Civil Rights struggle. While the first decision was taken in Dr. Martin Luther King, Jr.'s, Ebenezer Baptist Church in Atlanta, Georgia, in January 1957, it was reconfirmed in the Rev. A. L. Davis's New Zion Baptist Church in New Orleans in February 1957, giving New Orleans reason to claim itself the birthplace of the SCLC.

6. I've Known Rivers was a nonprofit organization that established an Afro-American pavilion of the same name at the 1984 Louisiana World Exposition.

7. The Ochsner Foundation was established in 1944 as a graduate training facility in specialized fields of medicine and maintains its reputation as a center for doctor referrals throughout the South for patients needing advanced diagnosis and treatment.

8. Jacob Lawrence (1917-2000) was an American modernist painter who also taught at the University of Washington. By the age of twenty-three, he finished a series of sixties paintings depicting the northern movement of black Americans in search of jobs and hope. *Migration* is considered his most famous work.

Elizabeth Catlett, American sculptor and printmaker, born in 1915, currently lives and works in Cuernavaca, Mexico, with her husband, Mexican painter, Francisco Mora.

9. Elder Hostel Study-Tour Group, founded in Boston in 1975, is a not-for-profit organization that organizes educational and travel programs for adults age fifty-five and over.

CHAPTER 6

1. (*Plessy v. Ferguson*, 1896) Homer Plessy, a New Orleans Creole, activist, challenged the segregation of passengers on trains that crossed state borders, an act that resulted in the widely adopted "separate but equal" doctrine.

2. See note 5, chapter 4.

3. Louisiana, *R. S.* 4:451 (1956).

4. *Louisiana Weekly,* October 14, 1961.

5. Kim Lacy Rogers, *Righteous Lives: Narrations of the New Orleans Civil Rights Movement* (New York: New York University Press, 1993).

6. Available from www.nul.org/90th/history.html. Lester Granger served as chairman of the National Urban League from 1941 to 1961.

7. Katzman Norton et al., *A People and a Nation: A History of the United States, Fourth Edition* (Boston: Houghton Mifflin Company).

8. Available from www.tulane.edu).

9. See note 5 above. James Farmer was a principal founder of the Congress of Racial Equality and was considered one of the "Big Four," a group that included Martin Luther King, Jr., Whitney Young of the Urban League, and Roy Wilkins of the NAACP. The last surviving member of the group, Farmer died in 1999.

Leontine Goins Luke, an ordained minister, was active in the 1950s and 1960s in neighborhood organizations, voter-registrations drives, and black PTA organizations in New Orleans. She spent a week in nonviolent training at the Highlander School.

Virginia Durr was a former member of the Southern Conference Educational Fund. In March 1954, Mississippi senator James O. Eastland brought members of the Senate Internal Security Subcommittee to New Orleans to hold hearings on SCEF. The proceedings were volatile. Virginia Durr, a patrician Alabama liberal, refused to answer the committee's questions but occasionally powdered her nose as a gesture of contempt for Eastland and his colleagues. Her husband, Clifford Durr, an attorney who had defended loyalty-oath cases during the Truman administration, grew overwrought during the proceedings and collapsed.

10. Available from interview with Leah Chase, July 22, 1999.

11. Thomas A. Becnel, "With Benefit of Clergy: Catholic Church

Support for the National Agricultural Workers Union in Louisiana, 1948-1958" (Ph.D. diss., Louisiana State University and A&M College, 1963), 131, 164, 201. The exact date of this meeting is unknown, but it corresponded with the movement among workers on sugar plantations to unionize, aided largely by the Catholic church. In December 1952, the National Agricultural Workers Union approached the big sugar interests, particularly Godchaux Sugar Refinery, requesting a session to discuss wage-claim forms. The Louisiana cane-field strike, the first clash between planters and laborers since the 1880s, occurred in 1953: "On October 16, 1953, the NAWU . . . placed ten pickets at the Godchaux refinery at Raceland in Lafourche Parish.

12. Keith Weldon Medley, "Dryades Street: Oretha Castle Haley Boulevard." *New Orleans Tribune*, April 2001, 19-20. Dryades Street was created from the Delroy-Sarpy Plantation in 1806 and is located in the central city historic district of New Orleans. Now named Oretha Castle Haley Boulevard, the street and neighborhood were developed by bold entrepreneurs of different religions, races, and classes, and, by 1930, was an entertainment and shopping alternative to Canal Street.

13. See note 5 above.

14. "Mardi Gras Blackout: Idea Gets Solid Backing," *Louisiana Weekly*, February 4, 1961.

15. A second line consists of a group of people who follow a jazz parade, sashaying and carrying umbrellas or flipping handkerchiefs.

16. "Blackout Isolates Zulus," *Louisiana Weekly*, February 18, 1961.

17. Social and pleasure clubs formed in New Orleans to help fulfill such functions as giving mutual aid, benevolent action, community service, and social outlets for its members. The Bunch Club was one among these.

CHAPTER 7

1. Norton, *A People and a Nation*, 489. The Works Projects Administration—which ultimately employed more than 8.5 million people and built more than 650,000 miles of highways and roads, 125,000 public buildings, etc.—was a part of the Second New Deal under President Roosevelt in 1936.

2.   The Flint-Goodridge Hospital formally opened in October 1896 as the Phillis Wheatley Sanitarium and Training School for Negro Nurses. In 1930, New Orleans University and Straight College merged into Dillard University. Flint-Goodridge Hospital of Dillard University moved into its new plant in February 1932 and was one of the few black institutions offering training for nurse anesthetists.

LINKS was started in Philadelphia by Sarah Scott and Margaret Hawkins, two African-American women, in June 1949. "When a woman becomes a LINK she becomes a link in a chain of friendship and makes a commitment, not only to members . . . but to every woman and child in the African American Community." *LINKS, Inc., Directory,* 1995.

3.   Community leader and wife of Judge Ortique.

4.   Joan B. Garvey and Mary Lou Widmer, *Beautiful Crescent, A History of New Orleans* (New Orleans: Garmer Press, 1982). The Superdome, built at a cost of $161 million, officially opened with a football game in 1975 and was considered, at the time, with a seating capacity of 72,000 for stadium events, the most extravagant building in the United States. It's completion and the arrival of the Saints professional football team launched a new tourism industry in the city.

CHAPTER 8

1.   Hirsch and Logsdon, *Creole New Orleans,* 302. Israel Augustine was elected judge in 1970 with notable biracial support.

Louisiana congresswoman Lindy Boggs took the office of her deceased husband, Democratic congressman Hale Boggs, serving from 1973 to 1993. She was appointed ambassador to the Vatican during the Clinton administration.

2.   Kim Lacy Rogers, *Righteous Lives,* 187-88. The Free Southern Theater was first an interracial, then all-black troupe that emerged from the Civil Rights movement in 1964. It toured communities throughout the Deep South, dramatizing material such as *Purlie Victorious* and *In White America.* In 1965 the FST settled in New Orleans and continued to operate, although under difficult financial circumstances, under the leadership of Tom Dent.

3.   Liberty Bank and Trust, one of the top minority-owned banks in the nation, was founded in New Orleans in 1972.

4. Donald E. Devore and Joseph Logsdon, *Crescent City Schools* (Lafayette: The Center for Louisiana Studies, University of Southwestern Louisiana, 1991). Rose Loving was elected to the New Orleans School Board in 1976, the first black woman elected to a citywide office.

5. The Schomburg Collection, currently, the Schomburg Center for Research in Black Culture, is with the New York City Public Library.

6. Clifton G. Webb is a New Orleans artist/sculptor whose work has been exhibited locally, nationally, and internationally, and has done much to foster the arts in the community through his volunteer activities. Mr. Webb was a founding member of the Contemporary Arts Center (which opened in 1976 as a center for artists' painting, theater, photography, performance art, dance, music, video, sculpture, and education) and is a board member of KIDSMART.

John Scott, born in 1940, is a Louisiana sculptor and teaches at Xavier University in New Orleans. He was the recipient of the McArthur Foundation Award in 1992.

7. Martin Payton, born 1948, is a New Orleans sculptor and teaches at Southern University in Baton Rouge. He was given a twenty-year respective at the Amistad Research Center at Tulane University.

David Clyde Driskell, born in 1931, is an award-winning American painter, printmaker, and sculptor who served as chairman of the Art Department of the University of Maryland from 1978 to 1983 and is currently professor of art at the University of Maryland, curator of the Aaron Douglas Collection, the Amistad Research Center, and curator of the Cosby Collection of Fine Arts.

Raymond Jennings Saunders, born in 1934, is an American painter and mixed-media artist who has won the Prix de Rome and National Endowment for the Arts Awards, as well as receiving a Guggenheim Fellowship and other awards.

8. Testimony of Leah Chase on FY1995 Appropriations for the National Endowment for the Arts to Subcommittee on Interior and Related Agencies, Appropriations Committee, U.S. House of Representatives, May 3, 1994.

9. Leah Chase celebrated her seventy-fifth birthday as a fundraiser for the New Orleans Museum of Art. Guests paid seventy-five dollars each to attend, she prepared the food and drink,

and the money went toward the purchase of a sculpture by Barbara Chase Ribould, now housed in the museum.

CHAPTER 9

1. Charlie Hutchinson (1921-1995), born in Madisonville, Louisiana, was one of the most innovative duck carvers ever in the state of Louisiana. He studied taxidermy specimens to define the detail in his carvings. Around 1980, he realized a record-high price, $23,500, for one of his carvings, which depicted a full-size pair of bald eagles hovering over a swimming channel of bass.

2. David E. Peralta, "Organized Labor in the Criminal Justice System: Mardi Gras and the New Orleans Police Department" (University of New Orleans, 1993), 26, 40, 57, 59, 63.

3. Arthur Burton LaCour, *New Orleans Masquerade, Chronicles of Carnival* (Gretna, LA.: Pelican Publishing, 1957). In 1872, upon hearing His Imperial Highness the Grand Duke Alexis of the Russian Empire would be visiting New Orleans, a group of leading citizens organized the Rex Association, adopting REX as a pseudonym. King of Carnival was launched and the royal Rex colors—purple, gold and green—became the symbols of Carnival.

The Mistick Krewe of Comus, which began in 1857, launched the "real" New Orleans Carnival, as it is known today.

4. Leonard V. Huber, *New Orleans: A Pictorial History* (Gretna, LA: Pelican Publishing, 1991). Gallier Hall, a Greek Revival structure, was designed by James Gallier and constructed between 1845 and 1850. It was dedicated as the city hall on May 10, 1853.

5. Anne G. Ritchie, *Women in Journalism* (Washington, D.C.: Washington Press Club Foundation, 1993). Iris Kelso, a journalist who began her career in New Orleans in 1951 at the *New Orleans State* (later to become the *New Orleans States-Item* and then the *New Orleans Times-Picayune*), began covering politics in 1954 when Chep Morrison was mayor of New Orleans. She left journalism in 1965 to work for Total Community Action and later joined WDSU Television.

6. Lawrence Douglas Wilder, elected to office in Virginia in 1989 and inaugurated in January 1990, was the first African-American to be elected governor of a state.

CHAPTER 10

1. James H. Dorman, ed., *Creoles of Color of the Gulf South* (Knoxville: University of Tennessee Press, 1996).

2. Gwendolyn Midlo Hall, "The Formation of Afro-Creole Cuture" in *Creole New Orleans* (Baton Rouge: Louisiana State University Press, 1992).

3. One early suburb *(faubourg)* of New Orleans was called Treme and was developed in 1812 from an old plantation to house an overflow of families from the Creole section of the city. Free people of color constructed homes side by side with white residents. Treme remains a mixed neighborhood but is largely known as a Creole community.

4. United States Department of the Interior, National Park Service, Denver Service Center, *New Orleans Jazz, Special Resource Study* April 1993. Uptown and Downtown New Orleans have and have had mixed definitions over the years but one point remains fixed. Canal Street divides Uptown from Downtown, with all streets beginning from Canal Street in either direction, numbered from 100 up. Divided according to their historical relevance to jazz, historic Downtown neighborhoods are Treme and the Sixth, Seventh, Eighth, and Ninth Wards. By the same criteria, Uptown neighborhoods are Mid-City, the Irish Channel, Jefferson City, Gert Town, Carrollton, and Black Pearl.

Jerah Johnson, "Jim Crow Laws of the 1890s and the Origins of New Orleans Jazz: Correction of an Error," *Popular Music* 2000. Traditionally, Uptown blacks were thought to be darker skinned and Protestant, while Downtown blacks were lighter skinned and Catholic. A different analysis is that the difference was cultural with no color, class, or status differences.

5. Nathaniel Burton and Rudy Lombard, *Creole Feast* (New York: Random House, 1978).

CHAPTER 12

1. A magnet school is a district-wide school organized around one theme or subject and is open to students from all over the school district, usually through a competitive application process.

2. In 1989 civic leader and head of Taylor Energy, Pat Taylor introduced a bill in the Louisiana legislature called the Taylor Plan. It would provide every student from a family making $25,000 or less annual income, but who had completed the core high school curriculum with a 2.5 average and scored eighteen on the ACT test,

full college tuition in the public universities of Louisiana. The legislature deferred the bill. The Louisiana NAACP called a press conference at the Dooky Chase Restaurant.

3. See note 3 chapter 8. The Boston Club is reputedly the second-oldest club in the United States, founded in 1841 by a group of businessmen who wanted more privacy for playing Boston, a popular card game of the times. Membership was limited to 400 males. The Boston Club hosts the Queen of Carnival each Mardi Gras.

4. Anatol Schenker, *Classics 704* March 1993) Blue Lu Barker was born on November 13, 1913, into a musical family and began singing at the age of seven in local clubs and at parties. In 1930, she married guitarist Danny Barker, who played with many of the best big bands of the thirties, notably with Lucky Millinder and Cab Calloway. After moving to New York, she cut a number of records with her husband, particularly from 1938 to 1949.

Danny Barker, *A Life In Jazz* (New York: Oxford University Press, 1984). Her song, "Don't You Feel My Legs," was composed by Danny and was considered risqué at the time.

Bibliography

BOOKS

Boggs, Lindy, and Katherine Hatch. *Washington Through a Purple Veil: Memoirs of a Southern Woman.* New York City: Harcourt, Brace, 1994.

Brown, Nathaniel, and Rudy Lombard. *Creole Feast.* New York City: Random House, 1978.

Chase, Leah. *The Dooky Chase Cookbook.* Gretna, LA: Pelican Publishing, 1990.

Dorman, James H. *Creoles of Color of the Gulf South.* Knoxville: University of Tennessee Press, 1996.

Gehman, Mary. *The Free People of Color of New Orleans.* New Orleans: Margaret Media, 1994.

Graham, Lawrence Otis. *Our Kind of People: Inside America's Black Upper Class.* New York City: Harper Collins Publishers, 1999.

Hirsch, Arnold R., and Joseph Logsdon. *Creole New Orleans: Race and Americanization.* Baton Rouge: Louisiana State University Press, 1992.

Norton, Katzman et al. *A People and A Nation: A History of the United States.* Boston: Houghton Mifflin, 1996.

Riggs, Thomas, ed. *St. James Guide to Black Artists.* Farmington Hills: Gale Group, 1997.

Rogers, Kim Lacy. *Righteous Lives: Narratives of the New Orleans Civil Rights Movement.* New York: New York University Press, 1993.

NEWSPAPERS

New York Times, June 27, 1990.
New Orleans Times-Picayune, 1945-2002.

Louisiana Weekly, 1930-2002.
New Orleans Tribune, 1985-2002.

MAGAZINES

Elie, Lolis E. "New Orleans Original." *Gourmet,* February 2000, 104-7.

Journal of the American Chef's Federation, 1998.Levine, Ed. "Food Is What We're All About." *Business Week,* March 2000, 240.

Manhalla, Christine L. "Personal." *New Orleans Magazine,* September 1999, 11.

Peck, Reese. "Back to the Basics with Leah Chase." *(New Orleans Times-Picayune) TV Focus,* January 2000, 9.

INTERVIEWS

Deloras Aaron—longtime personal friend.

John Bullard—director at New Orleans Museum of Art.

Bernard Charbonnet—attorney.

Leah Chase

Mrs. Jessie Dent—widow of Dr. Albert Dent, president of Dillard University.

Bill Fagaly—retired, New Orleans Museum of Art.

John Folse—chef and owner of John Folse Company.

Angela Hill—news anchor and former hostess of the *Angela Hill Show.*

Manuella Hutchinson—friend and widow of woodcarver artist Charlie Hutchinson.

Father Michael Jacques—priest at St. Peter Claver Catholic Church.

Dr. Andrea Jefferson—former vice president of academic affairs at Southern University.

Stella Jones—owner of the Stella Jones Gallery.

Brian Lanker—author and photographer of *I Dream a World.*

Sharon Litwin—former director of development at New Orleans Museum of Art, current director of the Louisiana Philharmonic Orchestra.

Dr. Rudy Lombard—former Freedom Rider.

Sybil Morial—widow of former mayor Dutch Morial, currently director of university relations.

Sunny Normand—friend.

Cleo Robinson—niece and sous-chef.

Cecile Rousseau—old friend of the family.

Don Rousselle—friend and producer of Leah's PBS cooking show.

John Scott—New Orleans artist.

Siblings, children, and grandchildren of Leah Chase

Jerome Smith—former Freedom Rider.

Dr./Col. Richard Stillman—professor emeritus of history at University of New Orleans.

Beth Strode—daughter of Celestine Cook.

Pat Taylor—owner of Taylor Energy.

Cliff Webb—New Orleans artist.

Alice Rae Yelen—assistant to the director at the New Orleans Museum of Art.

VIDEO RECORDINGS

New Orleans Museum of Art. *I Dream a World: Portraits of Black Women Who Changed America Exhibition*. Production of the NOMA and the Center for Instructional Media and Technology, New Orleans Public Schools, 1992.

WWL Television, New Orleans. *The Angela Hill Show: Leah Chase*, 1990.

WWL Television, New Orleans. *The Angela Hill Show: Moms and Daughters*, 1989.

WWL Television, New Orleans. *The Angela Hill Show: Shades of Black*. Part I of II, 1990

WDSU Television, New Orleans. *The Alec Gifford Show: Alec's Kitchen*, 1999.

Index